GURU NANAK

THE THINKER AND THE POET

Astri Ghosh is a journalist, translator and editor based in India and Norway, who works in Hindi, Urdu, Bengali and Norwegian as well as other Scandinavian languages. After working as a radio journalist for many years, she turned to translation and has published ten books in translation besides contributing to several anthologies. She grew up in Delhi and Mussoorie, moving to Norway to study at the University of Oslo. She now lives in Panjim, Goa, where she translates, writes and teaches. A few of the authors she has translated are Qurratulain Hyder, Rabindranath Tagore, Lars Saabye Christensen and Per Petterson. In *Sanger fra Adigranth* she translated a collection of hymns from Sikh scriptures to Norwegian.

She is currently translating twelve contemporary plays by Henrik Ibsen, four of which were published in 2015. She is also translating a crime novel by Jo Nesbø and children's books by Rui Zink. She does poetry performances based on poetry in translation, organizes jazz festivals and curates art exhibitions.

GURU NANAK

WHAT GURU NANAK DID, WHAT GURU NANAK SAID
THE THINKER AND THE POET

Edited by Astri Ghosh

hachette INDIA

First published in 2016 by Hachette India
(Registered name: Hachette Book Publishing India Pvt. Ltd)
An Hachette UK company
www.hachetteindia.com

SRD

ISBN 978-93-5195-049-3

Hachette Book Publishing India Pvt Ltd,
4th & 5th Floors, Corporate Centre,
Plot No. 94, Sector 44, Gurgaon 122003, India

Typeset in Goudy Old Style BT 10/13.5
By Eleven Arts, New Delhi

Printed and bound in India
by Manipal Technologies Limited, Manipal

Contents

What we know about Guru Nanak is through stories people have narrated down generations, through oral histories or 'Janamsakhis'. These stories give clues to events, but may not be exact histories, since they are influenced by the storytellers' own perceptions and background. When a story is passed on orally, it gradually changes over time. Each storyteller tries to put his or her personal stamp on the story. The editor of this book has tried to select the most significant of events from these histories about Guru Nanak, and those most relevant to Guru Nanak's teachings and to the readers.

Everyone Is Ill

The food was ready, but Mata Tripta couldn't find her son. She asked her daughter if she knew where Nanak was.

'No, he is not here, Ma,' Bibi Nanaki, Nanak's sister, answered. 'When I was on my way home with water from the well, I saw some yogis sitting under the banyan tree outside the village. Maybe he has gone there.'

Nanak Dev's parents were worried. Earlier, he used to be out playing with his friends every day, but now he would not go and play *gilli-danda* or *kabaddi*, or fly kites with the other children nearby; nor was he up to mischief like other boys his age. He had stopped going to school and was not interested in his father's business. All he wanted to do was to be by himself, lost in his thoughts. The strange thing was, if any holy men came to their village, he would rush to meet them and sit with them for hours on end, but when people came to visit the family, he would disappear.

Nanak's mother knew that if there were holy men in the neighbourhood, her son would be sure to go and start talking to them – and even forget to eat. 'I don't know what to do with that child!' she sighed. 'Why can't he behave like other boys his age?' She doted on Nanak, but he did exasperate her sometimes.

When Nanak's father, Kalu Mehta, came home that evening, Mata Tripta told him that their son had forgotten to eat lunch again, and been lost in thought all afternoon. 'Can't you speak to a doctor and find out what the matter is?' she asked him.

Kalu Mehta went to meet the local doctor. He told the doctor that his son had stopped going to school, was not eating properly and behaving strangely. He and his wife were worried that something was seriously wrong with him. The doctor promised he would come home and examine Nanak Dev.

When the doctor came, he tried to take Nanak's pulse, but the boy pulled his arm away and asked the doctor what he was doing.

'I am taking your pulse to find out if you are ill,' the doctor said. 'Once I know what the sickness is, I will give you some medicine to cure you.'

Nanak told the doctor that only God could cure him. 'You know how to cure the body, but how will you get rid of my pain?' he asked the doctor. 'My soul aches because I want to be one with God. Everyone is ill, and nobody knows it. You have to understand and experience God in order to know him. You will only be able to help me when you are one with God, when you live the highest truth.'

The doctor was surprised to hear such wise words from a boy as young as Nanak. He saw that the boy's love for God was pure. When Nanak's parents asked him if there was a problem with their son, he told them to stop worrying. 'Your son is not sick,' the doctor said. 'He is healthier than any of us. He belongs to God, and will be fine.'

Nanak's parents were left bewildered and confused, because they found it hard to understand their child.

What Guru Nanak Said

They have called the doctor to feel my pulse,
But the naive doctor doesn't know the pain is in my heart!

In the village of the body, five thieves live,
Even though they have been warned
They still go out and steal;
He who keeps his soul safe from the three modes and
the ten passions is safe.

Focus on the All-Pervading, He who wears garlands of
the woods,
Let your rosary be chanting the Lord's Name;
The four Vedas cling to a God whose roots turn up and
branches bow down,
He who is awake in the love of the Supreme Lord
reaches the tree.

The coral tree is in my courtyard,
Truth its flowers, leaves and branches;
Meditate on the Pure Light,
Give up all entanglements.

Listen, seekers of Truth,
Nanak says, break the snare of Maya,

Think of the Lord,
That you will not be reborn once again.

He alone is the Guru, the Disciple,
The Doctor who can diagnose the illness,
Man should not get involved,
And can be a yogi while living at home.

He gives up lust, wrath, ego,
Greed, attachment and Maya;
With his mind focusing on the Eternal Lord,
He finds Him by the Guru's Grace.

Wisdom and Contemplation are gifts from God,
Demons turn white before him;
He tastes the honey of the Lotus of the Lord,
And is ever awake.

The Lotus is very deep,
Its roots are in the nether regions, all pervasive;
With the Guru's teaching I will not be reborn,
I will discard poison and taste nectar.

If a hundred moons were to rise and a thousand suns
to blaze,
Even with this brilliant light, without the Guru, all would
be dark.

If the Lord is merciful, one receives the true Guru in one's
heart
And his soul that wandered through millions of births,
to it the True Guru imparts the Word.
Listen, like the True Guru, no one is beneficent.
Receiving the Guru, we attain the Truth and lose our
self;
Yes, through Him, the essence of God's Truth is revealed
to us.
The very first pain is that of separation;
Then there is the pang of hunger for Him.
Also the pain which mighty Death can bring,
And the pain when illness consumes my body;
O foolish doctor, bring me no medicine.

O foolish doctor, bring me no medicine.
The pain remains, my body aches,
Don't give me medicine,
Brother, it has no effect.

O foolish doctor, bring me no medicine.
Sandalwood is valued for its fragrance,
Man is valued as long as there is breath in him;
When his breath leaves him, the body crumbles,
After that there is no use for medicine.

The body is bright and golden, the soul made pure,
If the essence of the Pure Name is in it,
All pain and sorrow leave
And man is saved by the True Name.

Pain is a poison, the Lord's Name an antidote,
Grind it in the mortar of contentment, with the pestle
of charity,
Take it every day, your body will not waste away;
At the last moment you will kill the messenger of Death,
Swallow such medicine, O fool,
Which will cure you of your sins.

Kingdoms, possessions and youth are all shadows;
When the chariots move
Neither body nor fame nor social status go with you,
It is day over there, night over here.

Of burnt offerings, feasts and reading the Puranas,
Whatever pleases God is acceptable.

A Thread beyond Life

The house was full of people. The smell of spices wafted through the air. Everyone had come to take part in a ceremony. Food was being prepared for a feast. Nanak's home had been decorated for a party and Hardayal, the family priest, was invited as well. Hardayal would come to the family to offer prayers on major occasions and events.

The midwife who looked after Mata Tripta during Nanak's birth was called Daulatan. It is said in the Janamsakhis that when Hardayal asked her the morning after Nanak was born whether the newborn baby had made a sound, she said his cry had been 'like the laughing voice of a wise man'.

However, now he was no longer a baby. During Nanak's time, when boys of upper castes reached a certain age, a ceremony would be held to mark that they were growing up. A pandit would give them a sacred cotton thread called a *janeu* that they would wear over a shoulder and across their chest and they would then be initiated into the rites of adulthood, reciting the Gayatri mantra and other verses.

Nanak was nine years old when his grandparents and parents invited their family and friends in the village to attend his *janeu* ceremony. This was a tradition in Nanak's family and they all wanted to celebrate that their son had come of age. As usual, Nanak was nowhere to be seen.

Nanak's friends and his sister went to look for him. When they found him, they brought him back to where all the people had gathered in his home. Nanak sat down in front of Hardayal the priest and all the guests, and the pandit began to explain what he was about to do.

The sacred thread consisted of three strands of cotton spun together and tied with a knot, and was worn to help one meditate and remember God. Because only upper-caste boys got *janeus*, if you wore one, others could see that you belonged to a high caste. Once a year you changed the thread, and if it broke before that, you would get another one that was blessed and made sacred. Hardayal said that by putting on the *janeu*, Nanak would be a great man in this life and be happy in his next one.

Nanak tried to stop the priest from putting the thread around his neck. 'What are you doing?' he asked and tried to wriggle away. 'Why are you putting this on me?'

'When you wear this sacred thread,' said the priest, 'you will be a true Brahmin. This thread will remind you of God and your teachers.'

'But I can remember God without a thread,' protested Nanak. 'What if it gets dirty or wet? What if it breaks? Panditji! In case you have an unbreakable sacred thread that can make a person kind, contented, honest and disciplined, put it on me and I will wear it. When people die, they leave their body and this sacred thread behind. Only the soul goes on. If you could give me something that will go along with my soul, I would wear that.'

The priest felt Nanak was being rude and got angry with him. He asked, 'What kind of thread would your soul take along?'

'Believing in God's Name brings honour,' Nanak answered. 'Praising Him is the true thread that you take with you and wear when you enter God's Court. It never gets worn out nor breaks.'

Sure enough, Nanak remembered God throughout his life, without wearing a sacred thread.

What Guru Nanak Said

Believing in the Lord's Name brings honour,
The Lord's Praise is the True Thread,
For this Pure Thread never breaks;
With it we are blessed in the Lord's Court.
Make mercy the cotton, contentment the thread,
Continence the knot, and truth the twist.
This is the sacred Thread of the Soul, O Brahmin,
Put it on me, if you have one on you,
For it does not break, nor is it soiled,
Nor burnt, nor wasted.
Blessed are those, Nanak,
Who wear it around their necks.

If only they knew the nature of God,
They would know how false these rituals are.
Says Nanak, one must meditate with deep faith;
How do you find the way without the True Guru?

There is no thread for the senses, no thread for women,
No thread for when your beards are spat upon,
There is no thread for the feet, no thread for the hands,
No thread for the tongue, no thread for the eyes.

TRUE PROFIT

Nanak's parents, Mata Tripta and her husband Kalu Mehta, lived in Talwandi, in an area of Punjab that is now part of Pakistan. Weary travellers and fakirs would stop and rest here during their wanderings, and Mata Tripta would welcome and look after all the passers-by.

Kalu Mehta, whose full name was Kalyan Chand Das Bedi, was also known as Kalidas Chandarana. He was a Hindu Khatri and worked as the *patwari* or accountant of crop revenue for the village of Talwandi, under Rai Bular Bhatti, a Muslim landlord of the area.

When Guru Nanak was a child, he would often go off on his own to meditate. As he grew older, his urge for meditation became stronger and he showed no interest in worldly things. His father was worried that Nanak was too cut off from his surroundings, so he decided to teach him skills that would help him become a successful businessman.

One day he gave Nanak twenty rupees, which was an enormous sum of money at the time, and asked him to go to the market at Chuharkhana, a nearby town, with one of his friends to buy some goods. Kalu Mehta instructed Nanak to then find someone who was interested in buying the merchandise from them, so that he could sell it to them at a profit. He would have to make more money than he had spent.

'Go and make a profit with the money I have given you,' he said, sending Nanak and his friend off to the market.

The two boys set off for Chuharkhana. On the way they passed through a thick forest. In the jungle, a few sadhus were sitting under a tree. Nanak loved to sit and talk with sadhus, so he stopped for a while and discovered that they had not eaten for several days. They were famished. God would provide for them, they told him. He remembered that his father had asked him to make a profit. What better profit could there be than feeding the hungry?

When they got to the market, Nanak bought some food and clothes with his money. Instead of looking for customers to whom he could sell his wares at a profit, Nanak rushed back to the woods where the holy men sat. He gave them the food and clothes he had bought, and sat and talked with them. He was really happy that he had met them and enjoyed the conversation he had with them. Then he asked them to leave the forest and return home to their normal lives.

When he got home that evening, his father was furious. He had given Nanak money to teach him business skills, so he would learn how to make a profit. But Nanak had gone and wasted all that money and an opportunity to learn something, by feeding and clothing people who neither paid him nor gave him anything in return! What had he found out about financial gain? Would he never learn?

Nanak was the apple of Mata Tripta's eye and she forgave him instantly. Kalu Mehta, however, was so annoyed that he wanted to punish Nanak, and Bibi Nanaki rushed to protect her younger brother.

Guru Nanak did not care about wealth or money, or about what people and society said and felt. But he knew that we should give what we can to people in need. In his view, serving sages and holy men was a good deed, no matter what it cost.

Nanak said, 'Father, you asked me to make a good bargain. That is what I did. We might not get any money in return, but we will be blessed. That is what true profit is about – serving others.'

What Guru Nanak Said

Make your mind the farmer, good deeds the farm,
Modesty the water, your body the field;
Let the Lord's Name be the seed, contentment the
plough, your poor clothes the fence,
With acts of love, your seed will sprout and you will see
your home will flourish.

Make age, ever wasting away, your shop,
Stock it with the wares of the True Name of God
Make awareness and thought your warehouse, and put
God's Name in that,
Deal with the Lord's dealers, earn your profits, and let
your mind rejoice.

Let your trade be listening to scripture, let truth be the
horses you load with it;
Gather merit for your expenses, don't leave it till tomorrow.
When you arrive in the land of the Formless One,
You will find peace in His Presence.

Let your service be to focus your consciousness
And let your occupation be to place faith in the Name;
Let your work be restraint from sin; only then will people
call you blessed.

O Nanak, the Lord shall look upon you with His glance
of grace and you shall be blessed with honour four
times over.

Trade, O you traders, take care of your merchandise,
Buy the goods that you can take with you,
The Buyer in the next world is wise, He will care for
the goods;
Brother, chant the Name of the Lord with all your mind.
If you bring along the Praise of the Lord, the Lord will
regard it with joy.
How shall they that do not deal in the Truth find peace?
If we deal in deceit, our body and mind turn false,
Like trapped deer, we suffer in great pain, and cry.
False coins are not sent to the Treasury, they see not
the Guru,
Fake ones have no status or honour.
No one wins by deception,
They who trade in deceit come and go without honour.
Nanak, teach your mind and praise your God through
the Guru's Word,
Those who are dyed in the Lord's Name are not
burdened by doubt;
Chanting the Name of the Lord brings profit,
It keeps the Fearless One in your heart.

One who knows the Immaculate One swallows death,
One who understands karma recognizes the Word,
He Himself knows, and He Himself realizes
This whole world is all His play.

He is the Banker and He is the Merchant,
He the Judge who judges all Himself,
He tests on His touchstone Himself,
He is the One who estimates the value.

Nanak, one knows not God's command, by which all
must die.
For me the harvest of the spring is the Lord's Name,
The Lord's Name is the harvest I gather in the autumn,
I have pledged my God to farm only His lands,
There are so many courts in the world, so many that
come and go;
Beggars all, they spend their whole lives begging.

Marriage and Family

Bibi Nanaki was very close to her little brother, Nanak Dev. She would play with him and help her mother look after him. Bibi Nanaki was the first person to recognize and understand Nanak's devout disposition and mystic temperament. She didn't think he was lazy and unreliable; instead, she felt her brother's character was unusually spiritual. She acknowledged Nanak as her guru and became his first disciple.

She was his protector, placating her parents when they lost their patience with Nanak, often intervening when her brother's detachment from the world made their father lose his temper. Bibi Nanaki stood by her brother, and supported and encouraged him steadfastly all her life.

Bibi Nanaki's parents arranged her marriage to Jai Ram of Sultanpur, which is in present-day Kapurthala. Her husband was in charge of overseeing the collection of revenue in the court of Nawab Daulat Khan Lodi, the Afghan governor of Jalandhar Doab (a region roughly corresponding to the area around the city between Beas and Sutlej rivers). Nanaki was only eleven years old at the time of her marriage and she stayed at home with her father's family till she was sixteen, after which she joined her husband's family in Sultanpur.

After his sister left home to be with her husband, Nanak missed her deeply and immersed himself in meditation. Nanak's father became even more exasperated that his son continued to show no inclination towards business. With Bibi Nanaki gone, their relationship grew even more tense.

In 1473, a girl was born in the village Pakhoke in district Gurdaspur in Punjab to Mool Chand Khatri and Chando Rani. Her father was a very religious Chona Khatri merchant, who was the tax collector of his village. The girl was named Sulakhani. In those days, girls did not go to school. They would stay home and learn cooking, sewing, embroidery and housekeeping.

Jai Ram, Nanak's brother-in-law, worked for Nawab Daulat Khan and would often visit Pakhoke village because of work. On one of his trips there, he talked to Mool Chand about whether Nanak and Sulakhani would make a suitable match for each other. Nanak and Sulakhani got engaged in 1485, and were married two years later in 1487 when Guru Nanak was eighteen years old and Sulakhani fourteen.

Nanak refused to follow conventional wedding rituals. He said they did not need to consult any horoscope and that the priests did not need to look for the right time of the day; any time would be an auspicious time for the wedding.

This alarmed Mool Chand so much that he decided that he would not allow his daughter to marry Nanak. Breaking off an engagement in those days was considered outrageous behaviour and it created a major scandal. Very soon the news spread to other villages and towns. Hearing that the engagement was called off, Bhandari, the father of a girl in Batala, asked if Nanak would marry his daughter instead.

However, Mool Chand did not want Nanak to marry Bhandari's daughter either. He thought people would say Nanak had rejected his daughter and that would be an insult to his family's honour.

Mool Chand invited Nanak over and arranged for the priests to discuss the marriage rituals with him. Nanak and the priests sat down next to a mud wall to talk. The wall had been damaged in the rains, so someone in Sulakhani's family was afraid it would fall on top of Nanak and the priests. An old woman came up to Nanak and warned him about the weakened wall.

But Nanak just smiled and said, 'This wall will not fall for centuries. The will of God shall prevail.' And believe it or not, the wall is still preserved within the Gurdwara Kandh Sahib and a celebration is held there every year on the anniversary of Guru Nanak's wedding.

In 1487, when they finally got married, the ceremony was not held according to traditional rituals. Guru Nanak and Sulakhani went around the ceremonial fire four times instead of the usual seven.

Nanak lived with Sulakhani in Sultanpur for fourteen years. Even though it was usual to live in a joint family, they lived in a house by themselves, neither with his family nor with hers. His sister Bibi Nanaki told people that her brother needed his own space since many people often came to listen to him preach.

Sulakhani cooked loads of food and washed stacks of dishes, feeding the crowds that came to listen to her husband, and she supported his mission by participating in singing hymns. She gave birth to two sons, Sri Chand and Lakhmi Chand. Nanak was involved with his family and gave them his love and attention.

What Guru Nanak Said

The Lord is like a lovely temple, studded with rubies
inside,
Pearls and diamonds without flaws, a fortress of gold;
How can I climb up the fortress to see Him, without a
ladder?
By meditating on the Lord through the Guru, I am happy.

The Guru is the ladder, the Guru is the raft,
The Guru is the boat that will take me to the Lord,
The Guru will carry me across the ocean, the Guru is the
shrine, the river;
If He wishes, I will bathe in the pool of truth, and become
radiant and pure.

He is called the most perfect of the perfect and sits on
His Perfect Throne,
Looks delightful in His Perfect Place, fulfils the hopes of
the hopeless,
O Nanak, if one could meet the Perfect One, why would
his virtues decrease?

How wonderful is Your creation, how great are Your gifts!
So many of Your creatures praise You day and night
How many forms and colours You have, castes both
high and low!

ALL YOURS

Nanak's older sister, Bibi Nanaki, was very fond of her brother. When she got married to Jai Ram, she moved from her father's home to a city called Sultanpur. She missed her brother and knew that he often got into trouble with his father, so she persuaded her father to let Nanak move to the city where she lived.

Nanak's brother-in-law Jai Ram introduced him to Daulat Khan Lodi. When Daulat Khan heard that Guru Nanak knew how to keep accounts and could read and write Persian, he appointed him as storekeeper in the state store of Sultanpur, known as the Modi Khana.

People would come to buy wheat at the store, and Nanak's job was to weigh it and give it to them. He worked in the store all day long, weighing out provisions according to the regulations laid down by the Nawab. He worked hard and he was very honest, so his boss liked him.

One day a customer was buying wheat in the store when he noticed a strange thing. Nanak was weighing out the wheat and counting measures. But when he came to thirteen, he would get stuck. He just kept saying *teraa, teraa*. Now the word *terah* means 'thirteen' in Punjabi, but it also means 'yours'. As he came to the number thirteen, Nanak would start thinking about God and how everything belonged to Him. *Sab teraa*, he would say. Everything is Yours. Over and over again.

Lost in his thoughts, thinking, 'Yours, O God . . . All Yours, all Yours, all Yours', Nanak would close his eyes, and with a smile on his lips, scoop out a lot more wheat than the customer had paid for.

Someone went to Daulat Khan and complained that Nanak was giving away the Nawab's wheat for free. He said, 'Nanak is a decent person, a good human being, but he wastes your wheat and is throwing away your money. He gives your wheat away with his eyes closed.'

Daulat Khan thought he should check what was going on. He came over to see for himself. Everything seemed perfectly normal when he arrived. The wheat was all there. Then he counted the money Nanak had collected. He looked at the accounts book and got all the wheat weighed. Then he checked the numbers again to see exactly how much wheat there should be.

Khan was very surprised with what he found. There was actually more wheat there than he had counted on! Not just the Nawab, but everyone was shocked, because it was nothing less than a miracle. They had noticed Nanak giving much more wheat than people paid for, but lo and behold! There was more than there should have been!

God protected Nanak. Every time Nanak was about to get in trouble, he was kept from harm because he was honest and devoted to God. The people of Sultanpur saw this and respected him for it.

What Guru Nanak Said

What scale, which weight, and which assessor shall I call
That can weigh Your glory or test Your magnificence, O Lord?
Which teacher shall I go to, to be taught Your wisdom?
Whom shall I ask to evaluate Your majesty?

O My Loved One, I know not your limits:
You who pervade the earth, the waters and the sky,
You Yourself who fill all,
My mind is the scale, consciousness the weights,
Your service is the assessor.
Deep within my heart I weigh, my Lord, so I can keep
my mind from wandering,
You alone are the balance, the weights, and the scale,
You Yourself the Weigher.
You see Yourself, You know Yourself, You are the seller
of Your virtues.

The True One absorbs those who merge with the Word,
When it pleases him, we get included intuitively;
The Light of the Lord pervades all three worlds
There is no other than Him.

We must serve Him whose servants we are.
Unknowable and mysterious, He is pleased by the Word;
The Creator is the Benefactor of His devotees
He forgives them, such is His greatness.

The True One gives and gives, his blessings never run short,
False people receive but deny Him even more.
They know not who their source is; not pleased with the truth,
They are taken in by the illusion of the Other.

The God-conscious stay awake night and day,
Through the Guru, they know the love of the True One,
The egocentric are robbed when they lie sleeping,
The God-conscious are safe and sound.

The false come and the false go,
Through life's night they practise falsehood;
They who are united through the Word go to God's court wearing robes of honour,
The Lord is in the mind of the God-conscious.

The false are cheated, robbed by robbers,
The garden barren and uncultivated;
Without the Name, nothing tastes sweet.
If you turn your back on God, you earn nothing but sorrow.

Collect the wealth of the Lord, O brother,
Serve the True Guru and remain in His shelter,
This wealth can't be stolen,
The Word keeps one awake and alert.

You are the One Creator, the Immaculate King,
You arrange the affairs of Your servant,
You are immortal, immovable, infinite, priceless,
Lord, eternal is your place.

In the blessed city of the body, a place sublime,
Five virtues reign supreme,
Above them the Immaculate Lord, the One Universal
Creator,
They are absorbed in a trance.

There are nine gates to the city of the body,
The Creator made them for each one of us,
Inside the tenth gate lives the Unfathomable One,
Revealed only when He wants us to know Him.

The Primal Lord is unaccountable, true is His court,
His command reigns, true is His seal,
Nanak, search your home and you'll find
The Name of God immanent in the soul.

The Lord is everywhere, immaculate, all-knowing,
He does justice and is in the Guru's wisdom,
Grabs lust and wrath by the neck and kills them,
Gets rid of ego and greed.

In the true place, the Formless One lives,
He who reflects on the Word recognizes Him,

He comes to live deep within the true mansion of His presence,
And coming and going come to an end.

Then his mind does not waver, nor does the wind drift him –
Such a yogi vibrates the unstruck sound of the Word,
The pure music of the five primal sounds resounds,
The Lord Himself plays divine music.

In fear of God, he becomes one with the Lord effortlessly,
Gives up ego, is imbued with the unstruck melody,
With the kohl of enlightenment, he knows the Immaculate One,
The Immaculate King is present everywhere.

God is eternal and imperishable, He destroys pain and fear,
He cures diseases and cuts the noose of death;
O Nanak, the Lord God is the destroyer of fear,
Meeting the Guru, the Lord God is found.

Three Days in the River

I n Nanak's time, the lives of Hindus and Muslims were bound closely. Nanak worked at the store in Sultanpur for many years, but as time went by, he spent a lot of time thinking about how human beings were divided by faith. He thought about the different ways people had of worshipping the Lord. He composed songs and put them to music.

Early in the morning around four o'clock, at the ambrosial time before sunrise called the 'Amrit Vela', Nanak would go to the Bein River for a bath. He would emerge from the water and sit under a tree on the riverbank and meditate, often with his friend Mardana. Then he would go to the store where he worked. But his life was about to change.

According to the Puratan Janamsakhi, when Nanak was thirty years old, he went to the Bein for his usual morning bath one day. He took off his clothes, folded them neatly and put them on the bank of the river. Then he went into the water.

He was gone for a very long time. For three days Mardana, Sulakhani, Bibi Nanaki and Jai Ram looked for him all over. Had he drowned? Had he crossed the river and disappeared into the forest? Where was he?

His friends, neighbours and other people who knew him joined the search. They started walking up and down the riverbank calling, 'Nanak, Nanak, where are you? Nanak, Nanak?'

The Nawab came to hear of Nanak's disappearance and asked for the river to be dredged. But there was still no sign of Nanak.

Nanak was in a trance, he was in union with God; he was oblivious to everything else. He heard the voice of God saying, 'Nanak, this is the cup of My Name. Drink it. I am with you. I bless you and those who will be your followers and take your name. Go and repeat My Name, and teach others to do the same. Don't let anything soil your mind. Be kind to everyone.'

Three days later Nanak came out of the river. People in Sultanpur were surprised to see him alive because by now everyone was convinced he had drowned. Some people thought he had been possessed by evil spirits and they called a priest to exorcise these spirits. Nanak was silent, yet radiant.

After a long time, he finally spoke, 'There are no Hindus or Muslims. Everyone is alike.' When people asked him what he meant, Nanak explained, 'All men are equal and they are judged not by which family or caste they belong to, or which religion they practise, but by what they do. A Muslim who does not act according to the will of Allah, is unkind. In the same way a Hindu who is without kindness and truth, is no true Hindu.'

Many people interpret his words to mean that he was reminding both Hindus and Muslims of the founding principles of their religions. Others think Nanak was pointing out that Hinduism and Islam have differences in the way they express their beliefs, but that all men are brothers who only imagine the divisions between them.

From that day on, people started to call him Guru Nanak. He decided to travel and spread his message to everyone that all men

Some say poor Nanak is a ghost, some say a demon,
Others again that he is a man.
Crazy Nanak is mad about his King, his Lord.
I know no one else but God.

When one is mad with the fear of God
And recognizes none other than One God;
One is known as mad when one does this one thing.
When one obeys the Master's order – in what else is
there wisdom?
When one loves the Lord and considers oneself bad
And the rest of the world good, one is called mad.

When the field is spoiled, where is the harvest heap?
Cursed are the lives of those who write God's Name and
sell it.

Wise and all-seeing, You are a river;
How can I, a fish, know Your limits?
Wherever I look, there You are;
If I were separated from You, I should burst.
I know neither the fisherman, nor his net.
When I am in sorrow, I remember You.
You are everywhere, though I thought You distant.
Whatever I do is in Your Presence;
You see my actions, yet I deny them.
I have not done Your work nor uttered Your Name;
Whatever You give, I eat.

There is no other door than Yours; to whose door shall
I go?
Nanak makes one plea –
My soul and body are all Yours;
You are near, You are far, and You are in between,
You see and hear, You created the world;
Whatever pleases Your will, says Nanak, that is acceptable.

Everyone has to account for themselves in the
Lord's Court,
Without good deeds, no one can be saved;
He who voices nothing but the Truth
Is not asked to account for himself in the afterlife.

Dark deeds turn your mind blind, the blind mind blinds
the body too,
When the stone is riven with cracks, can plastering with
mud make it whole?
When the dam collapses, no boat or raft carries one
across the bottomless waters.
Nanak says, without the True Name, boatfuls of men drown.
If one is a king of kings, with tonnes of gold and silver,
Multitudes of men with spears and horses, and bands
playing heavenly music,
When one has to cross the bottomless sea of fire and
water,
Where one cannot see the shore, and men and women cry,
That is when one sees who is a king and who a king
of kings.

We should worship God with a single mind; our actions
should be pure;
God loves those who love mankind.

Only a prayer that is performed with the mind and body
in full concentration is accepted at the door of the Lord.
Prayers performed without full concentration of mind are
acts of self-deception and hypocrisy.

To take what belongs to another is like eating pork or beef,
Our Guru, our teacher, stands by us if we do not eat
such meat;
Talking will not get you to heaven, salvation comes from
being truthful,
Adding spices to forbidden food doesn't make it
acceptable,
O Nanak, false talk will only get you falsehood.

If an educated person is a sinner, don't punish the
illiterate holy man,
The deeds you do give you the reputation you get,
Do not play a game that will bring you to ruin in the
Lord's Court;
Who is literate, who illiterate, will be judged in the life
beyond;
One who follows his own will, shall suffer in the life to come.

God is wise and all-knowing, He purges us of our pride,
Getting rid of the Other, the One reveals himself,
In the world of hope we keep detached,
Sing of the casteless Immaculate One.
Getting rid of the ego, He brings the peace of the Word,
He is wise who contemplates on his own self;
O Nanak, singing praises to the Lord brings merit,
In the congregation you find the fruit of truth.

Passing on the Tradition

Guru Nanak travelled across the area now comprising India, Tibet, Sri Lanka, the Arabian Peninsula and Iran on four great spiritual journeys. He visited the centres of all religions and met with and had discussions with head priests of various sects of Hinduism, Jainism, Buddhism, Zoroastrianism and Islam. He spoke in temples and mosques, and at several sacred pilgrim sites.

Wherever he went, Guru Nanak spoke out against meaningless religious rituals, pilgrimages, the caste system, the sacrifice of widows, and of all the other tenets that were to define his teachings. He never asked his listeners to follow him. He asked Muslims to be true Muslims and Hindus to be true Hindus.

At the end of the last of his great journeys, Nanak asked a wealthy follower to donate a large expanse of land. Here he built a town, and called it Kartarpur. The town was in Punjab on the banks of the River Ravi, where he preached for another fifteen years. Followers from all over came to settle in Kartarpur to listen, sing, or just be with him.

During this time, although his followers still remained Hindu, Muslim, or of the religion to which they were born, they became known as the Guru's disciples, or *sikhs*. It was here his followers began to refer to him as teacher, or guru.

Vand Chhako is one of the three main pillars of the teachings of Guru Nanak. It means one should share what one has with others in the community – wealth, food or water – and consume it together. The term also means to share one's wealth with others in the community, to give to charity, to distribute in *langar* (community meal) and to help those who need assistance. A true Sikh is expected to contribute at least ten per cent of his income to the poor or to a worthy cause. The other two pillars are Naam Japo (meditate on God's Name) and Kirat Karo (work hard and make an honest living).

The Guru told his followers that they should be family men or householders and not live in isolation far away from ordinary people. There were to be no priests or hermits. Nanak also established the common meal or *langar*, insisting that all people, whether rich or poor, Hindu or Muslim, of high caste or low caste, sit together while eating. All worked together, all owned the town. Here is where Lehna, later to be called Guru Angad, came to be with Guru Nanak. Guru Angad became the second Guru of the Sikhs after Nanak.

Babur, the founder of the Mughal empire, came to India at the invitation of Nawab Daulat Khan Lodi. Guru Nanak wrote four hymns about the invasion of India by Babur, that are known as Baburvani in Sikh literature.

There is a well-known legend about the meeting of Nanak and Babur. When Nanak met Babur (he lived from 1483 to 1530), the Emperor of India offered him a hukkah. Nanak said that he already had a pipe whose wonderful effects never wore off. Babur asked Nanak where he could find such a wonderful pipe, to which Nanak replied that God, the True Guru, was his intoxication.

What Guru Nanak Said

Fear of You is my hemp,
My consciousness the pouch that holds it;
I have become an intoxicated hermit.

My hands are my begging bowl,
I am hungry for the sight of You;
I beg at Your door, day after day.

I long for the sight of You,
My Lord, I beg at Your door,
Bless me with Your Grace.

Saffron, flowers, musk and gold
Adorn everyone's bodies
So does sandalwood, the Lord's devotees,
Make fragrant all who come to them.

No one abuses ghee or silk,
So the Lord loves devotees of any caste,
Nanak begs at the door of those
That bow down to Your Name.

He alone is a hermit, who practises abstention
And sees the immaculate God below and above,
Gathering the moon and the sun;
Then the wall of such a hermit's body does not fall.

Says yogi Gopichand: 'Our God is the embodiment of truth,
Yet the essence of reality has neither form nor shape.'

He who gathers God's riches, earns honour and righteousness,
But the riches that bring you pain are not your friends
They who gather material wealth are known as poor people, O God,
But they that have you in their hearts are oceans of virtue.

You gather wealth through pain, and when it disappears, it leaves you in pain;
Nanak says no one is ever fully satisfied without the Name of the Lord.
Beauty does not still your craving – the more you see the more you want;
Many are the pleasures of the flesh, but they all afflict us with pain.

Black Magic Woman

For a quarter of a century, in his four Udasis or travels, Guru Nanak travelled around 28,000 kilometres to many countries in Asia to spread the word of God. Mardana, his childhood friend who had not left his side all these years, set Nanak's songs to music and always went along with him, playing the *rabab*, a lute-like instrument.

Once they were in an area called Kamrup where people were then known for their interest in black magic. When Nanak reached the outskirts of the city of Dhanpur, he sat down under a tree and began meditating. Mardana went ahead into the city to find food and water.

At the city well Mardana started filling his vessels with water. Some girls there wondered where he had come from. They asked him who he was. But he did not speak their language, so when he answered they thought he sounded funny.

One of the girls said, 'Listen to him, he bleats like a sheep!'

Her friends giggled and another said, 'Let's turn him into one!' So she put a hex on the gullible Mardana by putting a thread around his neck. He went down on his knees and started to bleat. Other people who were standing around and watching, dissolved into laughter.

When Mardana did not get back in time, Guru Nanak sensed that something was wrong and he came looking for his companion.

The girls saw him coming and decided to turn him into an animal as well.

One of them tried to cast a spell on Guru Nanak. She said, 'Bark like a dog!' But nothing happened to Guru Nanak. The spell was reversed and she began barking like a dog instead. Another girl came to the defence of her friend and raised her arm to cast a different spell. Her arm froze in mid-air and she could not move it. The girls tried several other spells but whatever they tried to do turned right back on them.

This alarmed a woman who was watching what was going on. She ran to inform Nurshah, the queen of Kamrup and a famous sorceress known far and wide for her witchcraft. Nurshah arrived at the city well to see for herself. She was surprised to see that the spells the girls had cast had been blocked. She tried to help them, but even her magic did not work! Then she tried incantations against Guru Nanak but those had no effect either.

Finally, she gave up and said to Guru Nanak, 'You do know magic! O great magician, please free my sisters, accept me as your disciple and teach me your magic!'

Nanak freed the girls at once and explained that they were just bound by the consequences of their own witchcraft. Guru Nanak then said, 'Real magic is meditation on God.'

The queen of Kamrup fell at the Guru's feet. He told them to stop using their powers for mischief and instead use them to help people.

What Guru Nanak Said

We are good with words, but not good in our deeds,
Our minds are dark, but we look fair on the outside,
We imitate the ways of those who serve at the Lord's
door;
Accustomed to their Lord's love, they delight in it.
Powerless, even though they have power, they remain
humble;
Nanak, our lives become fruitful when we keep company
with them.

Leave lust and wrath and slander,
Abandon greed and possessiveness and be carefree;
Break the chains of doubt, and unattached,
Find the Lord's essence in yourself.

Like you see a flash of lightning at night,
See the Divine Light in yourself, night and day;
Bliss embodied, incomparably beautiful,
Seen by the perfect Guru's Grace.

Meet the Guru, God Himself will save you,
He placed the lamps of the sun and moon in the sky.

See the invisible Lord, stay absorbed in devotion, the
Lord pervades all three worlds.
Blessed with the nectar, desire and fear disappear;

One enters a state of inspired illumination and gets rid of one's self,
Practising the Immaculate Word, one becomes the highest of the high.

Infinite is the Name of the Invisible, Unfathomable Lord,
Sweet is the essence of the Beloved Name,
God, bless Nanak with Your praise in every age,
Even though I meditate on You, I do not find Your limits.

Within oneself one can find the jewel of Your Name,
Meditating on the Lord, the mind is comforted,
On that difficult path one can find the destroyer of fear,
One does not enter the womb again,
Through the Guru's Word, the yearning for devotion,
I beg for the treasure of the Lord's Name.

When it pleases God, He unites me with the Guru,
The Lord saves the whole world.
One who chants the Lord's chant, gets the True Guru's wisdom,
Death's messenger serves at his feet.
In the company of saints, his state and ways are holy,
He crosses the sea of existence.
With the Word of God, one crosses this sea of the world,
Maya that is inside burns away,
With the five arrows of virtue, death is killed,
Drawing the bow in the mind's sky.

How can the faithless learn of the Word?
Without knowing about the Word they come and go,
Nanak, the Gurmukh gets salvation,
Through perfect destiny he meets the Lord.

The Fearless True Guru is our protector,
Through devotion one receives the Guru-God,
Blissful music of the unstruck sound resounds,
When the Immaculate One is attained.

He is fearless who has no destiny preordained –
God reveals Himself through his wondrous nature,
He is detached, unborn and self-existent –
Nanak, attained through the Guru's Wisdom.

The True Guru knows our innermost being
He is fearless, who realizes God's Word.
He looks inside himself and finds God within,
His mind does not waver.

He is fearless in whom the Lord lives,
Day and night he delights in the Immaculate Name;
Nanak, one finds the Lord's praise in the congregation,
And easily becomes one with God.

Men and women are all born of flesh, so are kings and
emperors!
If all of them are going to hell, don't accept their gifts as
charity.

He who gives will go to hell, but he who receives the gifts will go to heaven?
You know nothing yourself and yet you teach others, how wise are you?
A thief robs a house and offers the loot to his ancestors,
In the world hereafter this is noticed, his ancestors are called thieves too,
The hands of the middleman are chopped off, this is the Lord's justice,
Nanak, that alone is received in the world hereafter, which one earns by hard work.

Nanak and the Boulder

One day, when Guru Nanak and Mardana had been on the road for a while, Mardana started to feel terribly thirsty. His mouth was parched and dry. Not a cloud was in sight. The sun was beating down on them and the sky was the clearest blue. When they came to Hasan Abdal, a village close to a hill near present-day Rawalpindi in Pakistan, on the west side of the mountains, Nanak sat down under a tree to rest, while Mardana went off to search for water.

It was a very hilly area. The villagers told him their wells and springs had run dry and the only source of water was a spring at the top of the hill. It was near the hut of a fakir called Aliyar Wali Kandhari.

Baba Wali Kandhari was a Sufi, a Muslim ascetic and mystic, who was born in 1476 in Kandahar in Afghanistan. In about 1498 he moved to Hasan Abdal and built a small house near a natural spring. The water here was very clear and so the people used to come to fetch drinking water from this spring. There was no other source of fresh drinking water nearby. Kandhari would preach to the village folk who came there. Soon he had built up a small community or *dera*.

Even though he was thirsty and exhausted, Mardana managed to climb up the slope. When he got to the top of the hill, Kandhari asked him who he was. Mardana told him he was travelling with Guru Nanak.

'You can have water, as long as you pay for it,' said Kandhari.

Mardana said, 'We have walked a long way, we don't have any money.'

The man replied, 'Sorry. If you don't want to pay, you can't have any water.'

Mardana walked down the hill and told Guru Nanak what the man had said. The Guru told him to go back and ask for some water in the name of God. But the man refused to give him any water. Mardana came back down again.

Guru Nanak said that a person should have three chances to do what is right. 'Go once more and ask him to share some water with us in the name of God.' So Mardana, for the third time, respectfully asked the man for some water.

The man said, 'I've heard your Guru can work miracles. Stop bothering me. Ask him to give you water.'

Guru Nanak and Mardana were thirsty and hot. Guru Nanak found a small stick and started digging. And suddenly a spring of pure, clear water burst forth. The villagers were overjoyed.

The greedy man could see them from the top of the hill. He looked into his own spring and realized that it was drying up and all the water was going to the spring at the bottom of the hill where the villagers had gathered around Guru Nanak. Kandhari began to seethe with anger.

He saw a huge boulder nearby. Pushing with all his strength, he managed to roll it down the hill towards Guru Nanak and the group near the spring. The people below saw it coming and ran to get out of its way. Guru Nanak, however, was now sitting peacefully and meditating.

He calmly reached one hand out to stop the huge boulder. Guru Nanak's hand left an imprint in the hard stone as if it were made of soft clay. Kandhari realized that what he had done was terrible and ran down to beg for Nanak's forgiveness.

The rock with the mark of the Guru's palm is still there. Now a beautiful Gurdwara, called Panja Sahib, has been built at the same place. The word 'Panja' means a handprint. Thousands of people visit the site and bathe in the cool waters of the spring that faith brought forth that day.

What Guru Nanak Said

The pitcher holds the water, can the pitcher be shaped
without water?
The mind is held by wisdom, how can one gather
wisdom without the Guru?

The Guru is the tree of contentment, which flowers in
faith,
Its fruit is knowledge, watered by the love of the Lord,
It remains evergreen and ripens through action and
contemplation;
Glorious is the tongue that tastes it, this is the Lord's gift
of gifts.

Conquer death in your life so you won't regret it later;
Vain is the world, how do I make you understand?
We do not love the Truth, get involved in disputes,
Over our heads stands the messenger of death;
This wild demon does us to death, as the Lord wills,
If it is in His will, we cherish the Lord's love in our minds;
We can't slow down for a moment when the cup is full.
Know the Truth, through the Grace of the Guru,
And be one with the Truth.

Deserts are not satisfied by rain, nor is fire slaked by
wood,
A king is not satisfied by his kingdoms, and the seas are
full but thirst for more,
Says Nanak, such is my thirst for the True Name,
I seek its company for ever and ever.

Know and enjoy the eternal love of your Great Master;
If you become one with the Name of the Lord,
You can even strike Yama in the face.

Enigmatic and beyond comprehension are You, True
Master, unknowable and infinite,
Oh Lord, You are the only Giver, the others come
begging at Your door;
Whoever serves You finds well-being, reflecting on the
wisdom of the Guru,
Others love Maya, such is Your Command,
Through the Guru's Word one praises You with love and
affection,
For without love there is no adoration, without the True
Guru no love;
You are the only God of all, everyone serves You, this
minstrel calls out,
O God, bless me with contentment, may Your True
Name be my support.

One who knows God within and without,
Who remains detached and brings home the wandering
mind;
Nanak, he has drunk the nectar of the True One,
who is over all three worlds.

Meeting Yogis

Once Nanak and Mardana visited a sacred site high in the Himalayas. The yogis living there were ascetics who lived the lives of hermits in caves and in the forest. They were curious when they saw new faces. Who were these new arrivals?

The ascetics thought they would test them. As Nanak and Mardana came close to a lake in the mountains, they started to hear strange noises. Grisly figures came out of nowhere and tried to scare them. Guru Nanak took no notice of them. Soon hermits appeared from the forest and caves nearby.

One yogi called Charpat asked, 'Have you come to stay here with us?'

Guru Nanak answered, 'Why should I join a group of people running away from the world?'

Charpat said, 'You seem pious, but if you really want to complete your spiritual journey, you will have to give up the world and your desires. Then you can be with us.'

Guru Nanak said, 'You have not renounced the world, you have fled it. The world is on fire. You know how to extinguish the blaze. But you don't.'

Charpat held out a pitcher and said, 'Could you please take this and fetch me some water from the lake?' Nanak took the jug and went to the lake, but when he got there, he found no water. The lake was full of rubies, diamonds and precious jewels, along with silver and gold.

Nanak came back to Charpat with an empty jug.

'Well,' said the yogi, 'did you get me some water?'

'I couldn't – there was no water in the lake,' answered Nanak.

Charpat was actually testing Nanak, and he had passed the test. He wasn't afraid of the spooky atmosphere or the creepy spectres, and he wasn't tempted by the gold, silver and jewels.

A yogi called Loharipa asked if Nanak could tell him where the door that led to the Lord was. Another ascetic asked him if he would like to dwell with them there. 'This is the way to true spirituality,' he proclaimed.

The Guru said, 'Let me ask you something: You have many spiritual abilities, you know how to levitate and float in the air, you know how to reveal matter, but has this brought you any closer to God?' The ascetic was reduced to silence for a moment.

Guru Nanak told them, 'Our Creator intended us to be in this world. We can renounce it while being in it. We must be God-conscious and give up our egos, lust, greed and possessiveness. We must live the lives of family men and help other people.'

The ascetics contradicted Nanak. They argued that the only way to God was by renouncing the world as they had. Some even threw rocks at him. But some ascetics were moved by Nanak's words and some were open to his teachings. Guru Nanak left the mountains after explaining his way to God to the yogis and continued on his journey.

What Guru Nanak Said

A yogi asks:
Where do we come from, where do we go? How will we
be pulled in?
He who reveals the meaning of the Word is the Guru,
who is objective.
How do we find the essence in that which is not visible?
How can we learn to love Him with the help of the Guru?
He Himself is the Listener, He Himself the Creator, share
your wisdom with us, O Nanak!

Nanak answers:
Through His command we come, through His command
we go,
Through His command we are pulled into His will.
Truth lives through the perfect Guru,
Through God's Word one achieves dignity.

We can wonder over the beginning,
The Absolute lived inside Himself;
Think of freedom from lust as the earrings of the Guru's
Wisdom,
The True One lives in each of our hearts.
Through the Word of the Guru one enters the Absolute,
Effortlessly one attains the Immaculate Essence.
O Nanak, the Sikh who seeks finds, he need not follow
any other path.

Wonderful is His will, one who admits this finds the way
to the Truth,
One who wipes out conceit gets rid of desire,
A true yogi is one who cherishes the True One within.

In a state of absolute existence
He revealed himself as the Perfect One;
From being the Formless One
He took on a form;
He who knows the True Guru
Achieves the highest position
And becomes one with the True Word.
One who admits that the One alone is true
Rids himself of the Other and ego;
Only he who understands the Guru's Word is a yogi,
In his heart blooms a lotus that casts a shine on him;
All-knowing is he who learns to die while he lives,
He feels the merciful Lord inside himself;
Nanak says, one who recognizes himself in all creatures
attains salvation.

Words don't make you a yogi,
But one who looks at all creation alike –
He is known as a true yogi.

O Nanak, die while you are alive – practise such yoga;
If, without blowing, the horn sounds within you, and you
are without fear,

Remaining spotless in the filth of the world – that is how to achieve yoga.

He whom the Lord blesses can receive the Truth;
Nanak, he alone is blessed with Glory in whom God's Word resounds.
All hearts are mine, says the Lord, I am in all hearts.
Who can explain this to one who has gone astray?
Who can take away the one to whom I show the path?
He, who is lost to me from the beginning,
Who can show him the way?

O Brahmin, make God your stone god, right conduct the rosary,
Chant the Lord's Name, build your boat and pray 'Lord have mercy',
Why water barren lands and waste your life,
The wall of mud will surely crumble, even if you plaster it,
Make your hands the wheel, the chain and the buckets,
Yoke your mind like a bullock to work the well;
Water your body with God's nectar, and God the Gardener will own you,
Make Lust and Wrath the shovels with which you weed your farm;
The more you dig, the more peace you will find.
O God, in Your mercy, a crane becomes a swan,
Prays Nanak, the slave of slaves, O God, have mercy.

Through the Wisdom of the Guru, one's mind bathes in
the waters of the Nectar Name
And finds the sixty-eight sacred shrines within;
In the Guru's Words lie the jewels of wisdom; whoever
seeks will find them,
There is no other sacred place like the Guru's,
the Guru is the pool of contentment and compassion.

The Guru is the clear blue river water, bathing in which
one rids oneself of the filth of evil,
When one finds the Guru and bathes in His Wisdom,
animals turn into gods;
The Guru is like sandalwood, the core of his heart is
suffused with the True Name,
Who makes fragrant the vegetation around Him; let us
be attached to the feet of such a one;
Through the Guru the life of the spirit wells up, and the
God-conscious enters heaven,
Through the Guru one merges in the Truth, through the
Guru one obtains the Pure State.

false prophets

I t was the year 1510. Nanak and Mardana walked to Puri (in present-day Odisha), stopping at Cuttack on the way. Nanak spoke to people along the way, discussing the caste system, superstitions and the hold religious heads had on ordinary people.

There was a learned man named Kalyug who was very wealthy. People often visited his *dera* or camp, asking him what the future held in store for them. Many rich people were not that interested in religion, but wanted to know about their lives both on earth as well as in the hereafter. They would reward him handsomely for what he told them.

Nanak and Mardana stopped at Kalyug's camp and saw him sitting with his eyes closed, surrounded by devotees. There was a small metal container placed in front of him, where people could come and put their offerings. He would close a nostril, breathe in through his other nostril, then open the former and exhale.

'I am in heaven, I can see Lord Vishnu,' Kalyug said. He pulled up his knee and shifted his weight and settled down again, cross-legged, in the lotus position.

His eyes were still shut, and so his devotees also closed their eyes and listened in rapt attention, as Kalyug told them about reaching Brahmapuri and seeing Lord Brahma. Then he told them he was visiting Shivpuri to get an audience with Lord Shiva.

'Close your eyes and open your minds,' Kalyug told his followers. 'See the glories of heaven through your mind's eye. Come with me . . . do you see me there, sitting at the feet of Lord Shiva?'

Nanak looked around and saw that everyone present had their eyes shut. He signalled to Mardana to pick up the metal vessel in front of Kalyug and hide it behind him in a bush.

When the pandit opened his eyes, he saw that the container that held all the money that the devotees had put in it, was missing. He was furious. 'Who took the money?' he asked loudly.

The people sitting there rose and crowded around their priest. Guru Nanak came up to him and said, 'Panditji, you could see Brahmapuri, Vishnupuri and Shivpuri a minute ago. Why don't you shut your eyes and travel around the universe to try to locate the pot of money too?'

This upset Kalyug even more. 'Who hid my pot?' he blustered.

One of the people there tried to calm him down. 'Panditji, you could see the gods in heaven, surely you must be able to find your pot.'

'Don't be taken in by people who sit with their eyes closed, or who shut their ears or noses,' said Guru Nanak. 'They are like herons, standing on one leg, but ready to pounce at fish and frogs. This man could see where the gods lived, but he could not see his pot of money, which was right behind him. Don't waste your life on such acts. Just think about God and meditate on His name. It will free you of worldly desires.'

Kalyug pandit was inspired by Guru Nanak's sermon and asked if he would stay at his *dera* for a while. Nanak and Mardana agreed, and the pandit changed his ways.

What Guru Nanak Said

This is not the time when people know the true way to yoga;
Places of worship are polluted, the world is about to drown.
In the age of Kali, the finest thing is the Lord's Name,
Some people try to fool the world by closing their eyes and holding their nostrils,
Closing their nostrils with their fingers, they claim to have seen three worlds,
But they can't even see what is behind them; what a strange lotus pose that is.

The pandit knows all creation is through air and water,
And fire too builds and supports the body,
But if he were to know the source from where the soul comes,
He would indeed be a pandit, awake and aware.

One knows not the nature of God, O mother,
And he, who sees Him not,
What can he know of Him?
How can he describe Him, O mother?

He is up in the sky, down below in the underworld,
What can I say of Him, let me understand . . .
He who utters the Name with the heart, not with the tongue,
Knows alone; who else can realize the Name?

He who says the Name not just with the tongue but with
the heart,
Knows alone if God's Grace is upon him;
He who is in tune with Him, night and day,
He alone is an awakened man, who is one with the
True One.

At the Altar of the Sky

When Guru Nanak was travelling to the east, he ended his first Udasi with a visit to Puri and returned to Punjab in 1506. Located in the state now called Odisha, Puri is one of the oldest cities in the eastern part of the country. The famous Jagannath temple here is about a thousand years old and was constructed by the kings Raja Anantavarman Chodagangadeva and Raja Tritiya Ananga Bhima Deva.

The main deity is Shri Krishna, called Lord Jagannatha in that temple. It is the only shrine in India where goddess Subhadra, the sister of Lord Krishna, is worshipped along with her brothers, Lord Jagannatha and Lord Balabhadra.

The Jagannath temple was one of the four most important temples of the time, along with Somnath, Badrinath and Vishwanath. They were called the *char dham* or the four seats or places of pilgrimage. People believed that the idol of Lord Jagannatha was sculpted by the architect of the gods and that it was installed at the temple by Lord Brahma himself.

It was the anniversary of the installation of the idol of Lord Jagannatha. Nanak and Mardana saw a huge gathering of people who were dragging a great sixteen-wheeled chariot made of stone. On the chariot was placed a figure of the Lord Jagannatha. This was the famous chariot-procession of Jagannath Puri.

Later that evening the priests stood in front of the idol at the temple with trays laden with many lit *diyas* or oil lamps, flowers, fans and incense. They started to perform the evening worship called the *aarti* as the sun was setting. Oil and ghee lamps were burning. They moved the tray with the lamps around the deity while the congregation sang in praise of Lord Jagannatha. The plate or lamp was said to acquire the power of the deity.

Guru Nanak watched the ceremony quietly.

The priests then went with the trays to all the people who stood watching. They cupped their downturned hands over the flame and then raised their palms to their forehead – a blessing, passed from the image of Lord Jagannatha to the flame, had now been carried to the devotee.

After the ceremony, one of the priests who had come to Nanak with the *aarti* tray earlier, came across to him again.

'Why did you not join our *aarti*?' the priest asked.

'I am watching another *aarti*, one being performed by nature at God's invisible altar,' replied Guru Nanak. And he caught hold of the priest's arm and took him away from the lights of the temple to the seashore nearby where they could look at the sky.

'Have a look at the sky,' Guru Nanak said and pointed at the stars. 'The sun and the moon are the lamps that are placed in the tray of the heavens. The tray is studded with pearls that are the stars in the sky. The fragrance of sandalwood that wafts from the Malay mountains is the incense, the winds are the fans, and the forests are the flowers.'

What Guru Nanak Said

The sky is the tray, the sun and moon the lamps,
The stars are the pearls studded in it,
The scent of sandalwood in the wind from the Malay
mountains Your incense,
And the forest Your flowers, O Lord of Light,
What worship is this, Your *aarti*, O Destroyer of Fear?
The unstruck sound plays and kettledrums sound,
You have a thousand eyes, yet not one eye,
You have a thousand forms and yet not one form,
You have a thousand lotus feet, and yet not one foot,
You have a thousand noses, yet not one nose,
I am fascinated by this play of Yours.

The light is in everyone, You are the Light,
It is Your light that shines in us all . . .

My soul longs for Your lotus feet,
Night and day I thirst for Them,
Grant Nanak, the thirsty bird, the water of Your mercy
That he may dwell in Your Name.

All pleasures that cause excitement are silenced,
As one accepts the Guru's Word and is in harmony with
the One,

Seeing the waters of the self on fire, one quenches the
flames,
But only he who has great fortune realizes this state.

Serving the True Guru, one gets rid of illusions,
One is awake, night and day, in harmony with the
True One;
One knows only God and no other but Him,
By serving the Giver of Bliss, one becomes spotless.

friendliness and Hospitality

Travelling through Bengal, Mardana and Nanak walked from village to village on foot. One day, after they had walked for very long, they saw a village in the distance. All they wanted was some food and water, and a place to rest. They were exhausted and felt they could not take another step. Just outside the hamlet, they met a few villagers.

Nanak stopped and said, 'We are travellers and have been on the road since daybreak. We are really hungry and tired. Could you possibly give us something to eat and a room to sleep in for the night?'

'Just go away,' snapped one of the villagers brusquely. 'We don't care what happens to travellers.'

They spoke to others in the village, but everyone replied in a similar gruff manner. The two then had to spend the night out in the open as no one would let them stay with them, and finally they fell asleep, hungry and weary.

Early next morning they woke up to sing hymns and recite prayers. After they had offered a prayer called an *ardas* or a supplication to God, Guru Nanak blessed the villagers, 'May the people in this village stay here comfortably forever.'

The two of them then set out on their journey once again. Mardana was very upset. He was furious at the people of the village. 'Why did Nanak have to bless such inhospitable people?' he mumbled to himself. But he did not say anything out loud.

As dusk was falling, they came to another village. The people of that village were very different. They welcomed everyone who came to their village with open arms, and so they were very kind and generous to Nanak and his friend as well. They served them delicious food. They made up comfortable beds for them to rest in.

In the morning when they rose, Nanak told his friend, 'Let us pray.' And they prayed to God for the good of everyone. Nanak ended the prayer by saying, 'May the people of this village spread to all corners of the country.'

That got Mardana upset all over again. This time, he didn't mutter and mumble, but said what he felt. 'I just can't understand you,' he told Guru Nanak. 'You wish that the good people be spread all over the country and ask that the unkind ones stay put. You curse the good ones and bless the bad ones.'

Guru Nanak said, 'Listen carefully, Mardana. I was not cursing the warm-hearted and kind people who received us so well. I hope that these good people scatter across the world and that they flourish wherever they go. They will influence everyone they meet and make them better people. The whole world will be happier. As for those people who were so inhospitable, if they were to travel, they would make others rude and unkind wherever they went. It is better for them to stay in their village and not travel.'

What Guru Nanak Said

Everyone calls You theirs, O Lord, anyone who doesn't
is plucked away,
Everyone is rewarded for their actions, their account is
adjusted accordingly;
When one is not going to stay on in this world, why ruin
yourself in pride?
Call no one bad, read these words, understand what I say –
Don't argue with fools.

If I had a hundred thousand tongues instead of one,
and the hundred thousand multiplied twenty times,
a hundred thousand times would I say, again and again –
the Lord of all people is One.

Know the truth, never speak evil of anyone. Never
quarrel with a fool or speak ill of others. Speak so that
your words win the respect of all. To speak ill is to be a fool.

Infatuation with Maya spreads all over the world . . .
One can own everything but God.

Let me chant, O God, as I tell
The beads of Your Name
And rise above pleasure and pain;
So detached may my devotion be.

O Treasure of virtue, I cannot find Your limits,
Through the True Word I have become one with You;
It is through You one is caught in coming and going;
Only they can Your devotees be, whose minds focus on
the truth.

One is blessed with the loving adoration of God through
the Guru,
It is through the Word one gets rid of one's ego;
One stops going out, the mind stays in its home
And one retains the Lord's Name in one's mind.

PuRe aND ImPuRe

When Nanak set out on another of his long trips in 1508, it was to promote his mission. This Udasi or trip focused primarily on visiting Hindu places of pilgrimage. It was the first day of Baisakh, a month Hindus considered sacred, when Nanak reached Haridwar from Kurukshetra. He set up camp on the banks of the River Ganga.

A sadhu, who had many followers, was also camping close by. People came from afar to meet him and talk to him.

Nanak knew that he was an imposter and only pretending to be a wise man, which is why Nanak camped there to expose the man's trickery. The hermit would go for a bath in the river early in the morning and then start to prepare his meals. He smeared a patch of ground with cowdung to purify it so he could use it as a *chauka*, a cooking place out in the open. He cleaned the firewood to purify it, then drew a line around the cooking place and lit the fire.

Nanak asked Mardana to get some burning embers from the sadhu so they could light their own fire. But when Mardana came close to his fire, the hermit turned livid with anger and started yelling at him, saying, 'You have dirtied my cooking place!' He lifted up a piece of burning wood from his fire and ran after Mardana to hit him.

Mardana ran all the way back to Nanak, with the sadhu giving chase, hot on his heels. Nanak asked the hermit why he was so furious, for Mardana had only asked him for some embers to light their fire.

The sadhu replied that the shadow of this *mirasi* or minstrel had fallen on his cooking place and polluted it.

'But Mardana is a human being like you and me,' said Nanak.

'No, he is not,' said the sadhu. Nanak explained to the sadhu that God was not bothered about rituals and all the outward show of piety. God lives in the heart of every human being.

'If your heart is full of cruelty, hatred, slander and anger for others, you won't find God there,' Guru Nanak said. 'Look for Him in the whole of mankind. Don't judge someone if you think they are of low caste. Those who possess pure hearts, imbibe noble thoughts and always remember the Great Creator, are pious. It is a person's deeds that determine whether he is a decent human being or not, not his caste.'

What Guru Nanak Said

A body of saffron, a tongue of jewels, breath like the
scent of sandalwood,
If one's face has been anointed at sixty-eight sacred
places and one's heart has the light of knowledge,
With that wisdom praise the True Name, the Treasure of
all virtues.
O Baba, any other knowledge is false.

Deceit, no matter how hard you practise, still remains deceit;
If people worship you and call you a seer,
If you have a fancy name and are famous for your
powers,
But God doesn't accept you in His Court, all this
adoration will be in vain.

No one can wipe out those whom God has appointed.
In their hearts is the Treasure of the Lord's Name, it is
apparent
They worship the Name, they believe in it, the Eternal
Truth,
When the body turns to dust, what happens to the soul?
All your cleverness gets burnt, you depart crying;
O Nanak, what happens to those who forget the Name
in the Court of the Lord?

Wisdom the Guru gives is the only eternal pilgrim spot
where one washes one's sins away,
O God, Supporter of the Earth, all I need is Your Name,
bless me with it.

The Flavour of Honest Labour

Bhai Lalo was a carpenter who had a workshop at Sayyadpur, a town now known as Aminabad in present-day Pakistan. Nanak and Mardana came walking into Sayyadpur one day, and when Lalo saw two holy men coming towards him, he put aside his work, set a *charpai* for them and asked them to sit down. Then he went to get them some lunch. Bhai Lalo was nearly seventeen years older than Guru Nanak.

Lalo's home was a simple, working-class home. The kitchen was regarded to be the purest and cleanest place in a house, so Lalo asked Nanak and Mardana to sit there and eat.

Nanak said, 'Bhai Lalo, every place is clean and pure for us. Don't worry, please bring the meal here.' So the food was brought out to where they were sitting and Mardana then divided it into three shares and they all ate together.

'This food is delicious, it tastes like nectar,' said Mardana. 'What is in it?'

'What you just tasted was the flavour of honesty and hard work,' said Nanak. 'This tastes better than any fancy meal.'

Nanak always said that honest, hard work was an essential part of one's duty to God, along with remembering and reciting God's name and sharing one's worldly wealth with others who are less well-off.

Malik Bhago was a government official in a high position in the city. One day while Nanak and Mardana were there, he invited people for a big feast. Nanak was asked to join in as well. But he turned down the invitation saying, 'We are fakirs, what will we do at your feast?'

But Malik Bhago was a persistent man, so Guru Nanak took Lalo with him and went to Malik Bhago's house. Malik Bhago's servants brought them water and laid a platter of flavoursome food in front of Nanak. But he did not eat it.

Malik Bhago said to Nanak in a surly manner, 'You ate in the house of a low-caste carpenter. I am offering you tasty food cooked in pure ghee at my party. Why do you refuse to eat it?'

'Your food is not good enough to eat,' answered Nanak, and opened the lunch they had brought with them in a little box. He picked up a piece of Lalo's dry maize roti. With his other hand he picked up a puri from the plate. He squeezed both breads. Drops of milk started to drip from the maize roti. But from his other hand, blood trickled from Malik Bhago's fried puris.

'Look, Malik Bhago,' Guru Nanak said, 'when you make money by exploiting and repressing the poor, it is like sucking their blood. Your food might be flavourful, but you are asking me to eat food made with the blood of poor people, and to avoid food as pure as milk. How can I do that?'

Malik Bhago did not know what to say.

The news spread that a guru who challenged caste and authority was in town. Many people came to listen to Guru Nanak's sermons. Lalo was blessed by Guru Nanak. He became a devout Sikh and preached the Guru's gospel to the people of Sayyadpur.

What Guru Nanak Said

If one admits there is impurity, then all people
everywhere are impure,
Worms thrive in cow dung and in wood;
Even if there are many grains, not one is without life,
Is water not life-giving, that makes everything verdant?
How can we protect life from impurity when impurity is in
our kitchen?
Nanak, impurity cannot be cleaned this way, only wisdom
can cleanse us.

The impurity of impurities is the illusion that one loves the
Other,
Birth and death are at His will, through His will one
comes and goes,
All food and drink are pure, He has blessed us with
sustenance,
O Nanak, the God-conscious who understand Him are
not impure.

When one dwells on the Word, one's mind rushes to
serve others,
One meditates, practises self-control, chants and
overcomes the ego,
On hearing God's Word, one becomes liberated
And through such pious conduct, one finds true bliss.

The Giver of Bliss makes sorrow disappear,
I cannot think of serving another;
I surrender my mind, body and riches to Him –
Nanak, I have tasted the essence of God.
Kingdoms, riches, beauty, caste and youth, all five are
great deceivers,
They have deceived the whole world, no one's honour is
safe from them,
But they get overpowered by those who seek the Guru's
feet,
Unfortunate, O Nanak, are the multitudes who are still
deceived by them.
He shapes the vessel Himself, and He fills it Himself,
Milk is poured into some, while others remain on the fire;
Some sleep on comfortable beds, while others keep a
watch,
Nanak, the Lord enhances those on whom he lavishes
His grace.

PRiDe anD HumiLity

The son of the Sultan of Aminabad fell ill. He had a high fever, his body ached and he did not want to eat. He cried all night, and tossed and turned, and could not sleep. It was a nasty sickness and it just would not go away. All kinds of doctors, *hakims* and *vaids* were summoned to the boy's bedroom, but no one could find a cure for the illness. His mother stayed up by his bedside, while his father fretted and fumed, and called for new doctors to see if they might have some medicine that would help the boy.

When the medicines of the *vaids* and *hakims* did not help, they tried calling fakirs and all manner of holy men. Somewhere along the line someone suggested calling Lalo, who knew a bit about herbal medicine. As it happened, Guru Nanak was in town when the Sultan ordered Bhai Lalo to come and treat his son. Both of them went to the Sultan's palace.

When they came to the room where the patient was lying in bed, the Sultan and his wife were sitting there.

'Find out what the matter is with my son and treat him immediately!' the Sultan snapped.

Nanak did not at all like the way in which the Sultan spoke to Lalo. He was being too arrogant. Lalo might have been a working-class man, but he knew his herbs and medicines.

'If you want somebody to do something for you, it might be better to try requesting him humbly,' said Nanak. 'No one responds well to stubborn commands. Why should they obey your orders?'

The Sultan's wife fell at Nanak's feet and begged for forgiveness.

'Please don't be upset,' she said. 'We were just so worried about our son, the words came out wrong.'

Nanak asked Lalo to go home and fetch bread and herbal medicine. In the meantime, Nanak sat and talked to the boy, calming him with his soothing voice. The boy had been surrounded by anxious people, his mother crying, his father getting more and more irritable. When he heard the tranquil voice of Nanak, he felt comforted.

When Lalo returned, they put the bread on a plate and served it to the boy. Nanak sat next to him and calmly asked him to eat it. The boy, who had been refusing to eat or drink anything, listened to Nanak and ate the bread with the medicine and drank some water.

The fever broke, and soon the Sultan's son was on his way to recovery. He started eating and drinking again, and was able to get out of bed after a few days.

This was nothing less than a miracle, because he had been so ill that his parents had nearly given up. The people of Aminabad considered his recovery a wonder. Everyone started talking about Lalo, and the fact that his medicine had cured the little boy.

It was around this time that Babur invaded India.

Many people flocked to listen to Nanak for solace and comfort. Nanak sang hymns he had composed, like 'As the Word of the Lord comes to me, so I voice it, O Lalo.' Mardana, as always, accompanied him on the *rabab*.

What Guru Nanak Said

Let understanding be your mother, contentment your
father,
Let Truth be your brother; these are special.
You want to say something, but cannot find the words,
No price can be put on His nature.

Let modesty and intuition be your in-laws,
Make good deeds your wife,
Union with the Holy One, your wedding date,
Dispassion your marriage;
Says Nanak, Truth will be your children,
Born of this union.

The simmal tree is straight as an arrow, very tall, very thick,
But the birds that perch on it in hope,
Leave disappointed.
Its fruits are tasteless, flowers disagreeable, leaves useless;
Sweetness and humility, Nanak,
Are the essence of integrity.
Everyone bows down to themselves,
No one bows down to another,
Weighed on a scale, the heavier bit goes down.
The sinner bows down twice as much as a deer hunter;
Bowing your head is not enough if your heart is impure.

The world is sick, His Name the cure,
Without the Truth dirt sticks to your mind,
Pure is the Guru's Word, ever lighting up everything,
A shrine to bathe in the Truth.
Dirt never sticks to the Truth, why try to wash it off?
If you wear a necklace of virtues,
Why cry for anything more?

Thinking emancipates, and one saves others,
Not needing to be reborn;
One becomes the philosopher's stone,
The great contemplator, pleasing to the True One.
In bliss, night and day, sorrows and sins taken away,
Finding the True Name one sees the Guru,
With the True Name in mind, no dirt sticks;
Meeting with the Lord, a True Friend, is the perfect holy
bath.

Nanak says, meditate on the True One;
If you are pure, you will find the True Lord.

Babur and Bloodshed

The Indo-Gangetic Plain in north India was ruled by Ibrahim Lodi of the Afghan Lodi dynasty, whereas Rajputana was ruled by a Hindu Rajput Confederacy, lead by Rana Sanga of Mewar. In 1524, Daulat Khan Lodi, who was a rebel of the Lodi dynasty, invited Babur to overthrow Ibrahim and become the ruler of India. Babur defeated Ibrahim Lodi at the First Battle of Panipat in 1526 and founded the Mughal empire. When Nanak was in Sayyadpur, Babur's soldiers rode through Punjab with fire and swords, bringing destruction and devastation all over, including the town where Nanak and Mardana were staying.

Weeping and wailing resounded as people were killed and homes plundered. Those who resisted were put to death. Riches were looted and women were taken away. People were struck with terror and there was no one to keep Babur's soldiers in check. Their cruelty was beyond belief. In the disorder, heaps of human bodies lay all over and the town was in ruins.

Guru Nanak looked around and saw the desolation in a town where people once had been very proud of their riches. He said, 'Wealth and riches are at the root of all this bloodshed. Those who commit evil deeds will suffer. Joy or sorrow are the fruits of one's own actions, nobody is to be blamed for them.'

Under the orders of Babur, everyone was arrested, put in prison and set to various tasks. Nanak and Mardana were also arrested and given corn to grind. But even when he was in prison, Nanak meditated. While he was lost in thought, the grinding stone turned by itself.

Babur got to hear about this miracle. He understood immediately that Nanak was a holy man. He begged for forgiveness and set Nanak free. But Nanak wasn't satisfied, and he asked Babur to free the rest of the prisoners as well, which Babur did.

Babur was pleased with Nanak and said, 'O wise man! Is there anything else you would like to ask for?'

Guru Nanak replied, 'God, who sustains every creature on this earth, has given me much more than I need. All kings are what they are due to His grace. Those that rely upon other men end up being losers.'

The people of Sayyadpur who had escaped alive returned to the town. They found many of their relatives missing or killed, and they were overwhelmed with grief.

Guru Nanak spoke to them about facing death. 'The people in whose fate it was to die, had to go. That was the will of God. Babur invaded because of the misdeeds of other rulers. Keeping our faith in God is our only help. If the people and the rulers do not change their ways, there will be more bloodshed. But they can't get away forever. Divine justice will befall those who do evil.'

What Guru Nanak Said

As the Word of the Lord comes to me, so I voice it, O
Lalo,
Babur comes from Kabul with his wedding party of sin,
bids us gift away our land;
Shame and righteousness have gone into hiding, while
deceit struts around like a leader,
The Qazi and Brahmin's days are over, the devil acts the
priest,
Muslim women read the Quran, in misery they call on
God, O Lalo,
Hindu women of all castes together have to do the
same, O Lalo,
Wedding songs of murder are sung while blood is
sprinkled instead of saffron,
Nanak sings praises to the Lord in this city of
destruction;
He who created all and gave them pleasures, sits and
watches,
True is the Master, true is His justice, true His command.
When the clothes from our bodies are torn to shreds,
Hindustan will remember,
Coming in seventy-eight, they will leave in ninety-seven,*
Another disciple and man will rise;

* The numbers refer to the dates of Babur's invasion of India, which Sikhs
believe Guru Nanak predicted.

Nanak speaks the Truth, now is the time to voice the Truth.

He who considers himself wise must be responsible for his deeds,
For without the Name, he is held to be false and has a difficult time;
His way is blocked, he finds no way to escape,
The man of contentment reaches the True God through the Word;
Deep, fathomless and profound is God, one cannot sound His depths,
Without the Guru, one is struck in the face and cannot be set free,
If one chants the Name of the Lord, one is blessed with honour in one's true home;
Know that God, through His will, blesses us with life and sustains us.

Kings and emperors with mountains of wealth
And oceans of riches
Are not as tall as an ant
That keeps God's Name in mind.

walking all over the world

Nanak was moved by the plight of people around him and he wanted to tell them about the 'real message of God'. He was committed to bringing his message to the masses, so in 1499, he decided to set out on his sacred mission to spread the holy message of peace and compassion to all of mankind.

When Nanak got married and his wife Bibi Sulakhani came to their home, Mata Tripta was thrilled and overjoyed. When Guru Nanak's first son, Sri Chand, was born, she distributed sweets among the village folk, and on the birth of her second grandson, Lakhmi Chand, she was so excited at becoming a grandmother again that she was happy beyond all description.

Even though she had her grandsons, when her son was out on his travels, Mata Tripta missed him desperately. But she always comforted Bibi Sulakhani and was a good mother-in-law to her.

In 1499 Nanak left Sultanpur, where he lived and worked, and went home to his village Talwandi to meet his parents and inform them about the long journey he was about to undertake.

His parents missed him and his family after Nanak moved to Sultanpur. They wanted their son to be near them in their old age and look after them, so they told him they would prefer that he did not go. Why didn't he move back to Talwandi? What was going to happen to his wife and his sons? Was he leaving them unprotected?

But Nanak said that thousands of people were waiting for the divine message of the Almighty for comfort, love and salvation.

Nanak told his parents, 'This is a call from heaven, I must go where He tells me to go.'

Hearing it put in such a way, his parents had no choice but to let him go and they gave him their blessings. So Nanak started his mission and the roots of Sikhism were laid. Most of his journeys were made on foot with his companion Mardana, the Muslim minstrel who played the *rabab*. Nanak travelled in all four directions – north, east, west and south. The first tour headed east towards Bengal, Assam and Manipur, the second south towards Sri Lanka, the third north towards present-day Kashmir, Ladakh, Tibet and Arunachal Pradesh, and on the final trip they went west towards Baghdad, Mecca and Medina on the Arabian Peninsula.

Although the exact account of his route is disputed, Nanak is widely believed to have made four major journeys, covering around 28,000 kilometres over a period of twenty-five years.

Nanak visited various centres of Hindus, Muslims, Buddhists, Jains, Sufis, Yogis and Siddhas. He met people of different religions, tribes, cultures and races.

When he came back from his first long trip, Nanak's parents met him at the edge of the village. Nanak was so overwhelmed at seeing his mother that he had tears in his eyes. She had brought him sweets, and she asked him to take off his tattered robes and put on the clothes she had carried for him. She loved her son dearly and wanted her friends and neighbours to see him in the best light possible.

His father, Kalu, once exclaimed, 'If only I knew what has disappointed you in life, I would set things right. Do you want to marry another woman? I can arrange another marriage for you. If you want another house, I will give you one.' His parents just could not understand Nanak's behaviour.

Nanak's parents believed that his travels and rejection of conventions were a sign of great unhappiness. His parents, who were well-to-do and highly respected in their community, were concerned because they did not understand why he would not conform to the social customs of the day.

When they went north, Nanak crossed into what is now called Arunachal Pradesh and visited many areas of the region. While going to Lhasa in Tibet, he passed through Tawang from Bhutan. Mardana and Nanak entered Tibet from Samdurang Chu. On their way back from Lhasa they went to the famous Samye monastery and then to Pemoshubu Menchukha in Arunachal Pradesh. Nanak meditated there for some time. From Menchukha he went back to Tibet, bringing some residents of southern Tibet with him to Menchukha. Then they left, going through Gelling and Tuting to Sadiya and Brahma-Kund, before once again entering the present-day state of Assam.

Once when Nanak returned from his travels and came to Talwandi, Mata Tripta knew she did not have much time left, so she beseeched him to stay there for a while. Guru Nanak touched her feet to receive her blessings, and she gave him one last loving embrace. She passed away in 1522. Guru Nanak performed her last rites himself, and told everyone that there was no need for any other rituals to be performed. He was convinced that if you develop your spirituality, you regard happy events and miserable events as one, because the will of God causes them. He asked the people to meditate on God's Name instead and to accept God's will.

What Guru Nanak Said

Speak the truth and you will live in the house of truth,
Die while you are alive and swim across the sea of existence.
The Guru is the boat, the ship the raft; meditate on Him
and go across.

Ego, greed and possessiveness are destroyed,
Set free from the nine gates, one enters the tenth
and sees the Transcendent One, Highest of the High,
born of Himself.

Accept the Guru's teachings and cross the sea in His love,
Singing praises to the Absolute One, why should I fear
death?
Wherever I look, I only see You, I sing of no other;
True is the Lord's Name, true His sanctuary.

True is the Guru's Word,
Clutching it one crosses over,
Speaking the unspoken, seeing the Infinite One,
One does not enter the womb again.

Without the truth, you can't find contentment,
Without the Guru, one cannot be set free;
Chanting the Mool Mantar* and the Name of the Lord,
Nanak says, I have found the Perfect One.

* This is said to be the first composition uttered by Guru Nanak Dev upon
enlightenment at the age of about thirty. It encapsulates the main principles
of Sikhism.

Without Truth, one cannot cross the sea of existence,
The sea is vast and unfathomable, filled to the brim with
poison;
Whoever receives the Guru's teaching and remains
detached,
He finds a place in the home of the Fearless God.

False is the cleverness of loving attachments of this world,
In no time at all they come and go;
Forgetting the Name, the proud egocentric ones leave,
In creation and destruction they waste away.

In creation and destruction they are bound in bondage,
The ego and Maya in a noose around their necks;
Whoever does not cherish the Guru's teachings and the
Name of the Lord,
Is bound and driven to the city of death.

Without the Guru, how can one be set free?
Without the Guru, how can one meditate?
Accept the Guru's teachings, cross the ocean,
You will be set free and find peace.

Through the Guru's wisdom, Krishna lifted Mount
Govardhan,
Through the Guru's wisdom, stones floated across the
ocean,

Accept the Guru's wisdom for the highest state of bliss,
Nanak, the Guru, rids you of your doubts.

Accept the Guru's wisdom, swim across to the other
side through truth,
O soul, cherish the Lord in your heart;
Death's noon is cut away, meditate on the Lord,
You will find the Immaculate One who has no caste.

Through the Guru's wisdom saints, friends and brothers
are united,
Through the Guru's wisdom, fire is quenched and
controlled.
Chant the Name with your mind and mouth,
Know the unknowable one deep in your heart.

The Gurmukh* understands and is pleased with the
Word,
Whom shall one praise or slight?
Know yourself, meditate on the Lord,
Let your mind be pleased by the Master of the Universe.

Know Him who is all the realms of the universe,
Know Him through the Guru and the Guru's Word,
He enjoys each and every heart,
But remains detached from everyone.

* God-conscious.

Praise the Lord with the Guru's Word,
See Him with your own eyes,
Listen to His Name and Word,
Be steeped in His love.

GURU Nanak's Beliefs and Teachings

Guru Nanak stressed that all human beings could have direct access to God without resorting to rituals or priests. He spoke against the caste system, setting up a spiritual, social and political platform based on equality, love, goodness and virtue.

He also rejected the path of asceticism and drew attention to how one could lead a family life without being very materialistic. Selfless service of mankind (*sewa*), singing hymns (*kirtan*), contemplation and meditation on God's name, in the company of other devoted people (*satsang*), and faith in 'One' Omnipotent God are some of the basic concepts of Sikhism established by Guru Nanak.

Nanak strongly believed in the equality of all human beings. He supported the causes of the oppressed and the poor, and asserted the right of women to be treated as equal citizens with men.

He was critical of the system of government of the Mughal rulers, and was arrested for challenging the acts of brutality of the Mughal emperor Babur. Guru Nanak was released, along with all other innocent captives, after Babur realized the error of his ways.

✦

Devoted to matters of the spirit, it is said Nanak was inspired by a powerful spiritual experience that gave him a vision of the true nature of God; this led him to preach that spiritual growth was achievable through contemplation and meditation, and through a way of living that demonstrated the presence of the divine within all human beings. He insisted that endeavours such as pilgrimages and penances were not as important as meditation.

✦

Nanak spoke of the dangers of egotism (*haumai*, which means 'I am') and asked his followers to worship through the Word of God. 'Naam' or the Lord's name is a mystical word to recite or meditate upon, through *hukam*, a guru's instructions. In the process of singing of God's qualities, one gets rid of doubt.

✦

The Word of God purifies a person and makes worship possible. Such worship must be selfless. Nanak warned against hypocrisy and falsehood, saying that these are widespread in humanity and that religious actions could often be in vain if those carrying them out were hypocritical or untrue in spirit. He did not favour asceticism, and suggested that one remain inwardly detached while leading a normal family life.

❧

Nanak's teaching is understood to be practised in the following three ways:

- Sharing with others, helping those who are in need
- Making a living honestly, without exploitation or fraud
- Meditating on God's name to control the five weaknesses

❧

Nanak put the greatest emphasis on the worship of the Word of God (Naam Japna). One should follow the direction of God-conscious, awakened individuals rather than of those who are led by self-will, as that would only lead to frustration.

❧

Nanak's teachings can be found in the Sikh sacred text, the Sri Guru Granth Sahib, in an extensive collection of verses recorded in Gurmukhi. The word 'Shabad' has two key meanings in Sikhism. It is used to refer to a hymn or paragraph in the Sri Guru Granth

Sahib, the main holy scripture of the Sikhs. It is organized by chapters of ragas, with each chapter containing many Shabads of that particular raga. The first Shabad in the Sri Guru Granth Sahib is the Mool Mantar. Shabad is also used to refer to hymns within other Sikh scriptures. Another use of the term Shabad within Sikhism is for the holy name of God, Waheguru.

The Japji Sahib

The Japji Sahib appears at the beginning of the holy scripture of the Sikhs, the Guru Granth Sahib, composed by Guru Nanak. It is headed by the Mool Mantar and followed by 38 Pauris (stanzas). At the end of the prayer there is a final Salok.

❧

The Japji Sahib is believed to be the first composition of Guru Nanak, and considered the essence of the Sikh faith. It is regarded amongst the most important Bani or 'set of verses' by the Sikhs, as it is the first Bani in the Nit-nem.

❧

'Japu' is to recite, to repeat, or to chant. But 'Jap' also means to understand wisdom. The Japji discusses the nature of God and what true worship is. It says that God is indescribable, that the only true form of worship is accepting God, and remaining one with Him. The 'Nit-Nem' (literally 'Daily Discipline') is a collection of selected hymns that Sikhs read every day at fixed times of the day. It normally includes the Gurbani, which is read daily by Sikhs in the morning, evening and at night.

Mool Mantar

There is one God –
Truth is His Name;
He is the creator,
Fearless, without hate,
He is eternal.
Free from the cycle of life and death
He exists by himself and can be realized
Through the grace of the Guru.

True in the beginning,
True through the ages,
True now,
Will always be True.

Japji Sahib

1

He cannot be known through thoughts
Though one might think
A hundred thousand times,
Or be still and meditate for long;
The hungry still hunger

Even with a pile of goods,
Even with a hundred thousand clever ways;
Not one will go with you to God.
How do we reach the Truth?
How do we remove
The veil of falsehood?
O Nanak, it is written,
Obey the Lord's will,
Follow the right path.

2
Everything is created at His command,
But His command cannot be described;
His command creates life
And His command is the way to greatness,
His command makes some high and others low;
The scriptures decide who gets joy or sorrow –
Some get rewarded, others wander endlessly
Through life and death;
All are under His command –
No one escapes;
O Nanak, the one who follows His command
Never says 'It is I.'

3
Some sing of His might –
Who has the strength to sing of His might?
Some sing of His gifts
And know His signs,

Some sing of His greatness
And His virtues,
Some sing of His knowledge
Though hard to comprehend,
Some sing that He creates the body
And turns it to dust,
Some sing He takes life
And gives it back.

Some sing that He is distant,
Others sing of His presence –
To describe the Lord is impossible
Though there is no lack of those who try;
Countless are the people
Who tell a million stories;
The Giver keeps giving –
We who receive grow weary,
Through the ages we live on His gifts –
God, with His command, leads us
Down the right path.
Carefree, says Nanak, God ever rejoices.

4
True is God,
True is His Name,
Endless love is His language;
His creatures beg and say,
Give, give,

And the Generous One gives;
What shall we offer
To see His court?
What words must we say
To win His love?

Praise His true Name –
Think of Him
In the ambrosial light of the morning;
Our past deeds determine our birth,
Only through His grace
Do we attain salvation;
Nanak says we must know this –
God is Truth itself.

5
God cannot be pictured,
No one can create Him;
He created Himself and is perfect –
Honoured are those that serve Him.

O Nanak, sing of the Lord,
The source of all excellence;
Sing, listen, fill your mind with His love,
So your pain disappears
And your heart is filled with joy.

The Word of the Guru is *nada*, the inner sound,
The Word of the Guru is the Vedas,

The Word of the Guru triumphs,
The Guru is Shiva, Vishnu and Brahma,
The Guru is Parvati and Lakshmi and Saraswati.

If I were to know God, I could not describe Him,
Are there any words to describe Him?
The Guru has given me this certainty –
There is only One, who gives life to everyone,
May I never forget Him.

6

I would bathe in holy rivers
To please Him,
Why go on a pilgrimage
If not to please Him?
This is the law of creation –
What does one gain without good deeds?
If you listen to the Guru,
You find jewels in the mind –
Gems and rubies.
This one command the
Guru has given –
All souls come from the One,
May I never forget Him.

7

If one could live through the four ages
And ten times that,
If one were known through nine parts of the world

And everyone followed you,
If your name was known all over the world
It would be of no use
If you did not have God's grace.
You would be the lowest of the low,
Even the most pitiful sinners would despise you.
God blesses the unworthy with virtues, O Nanak,
The virtuous with virtue.
There is none one could imagine
That would give God virtues.

8

By listening to God's Word
One becomes a *siddha*, a sufi or a yogi,
By listening to God's Word
One learns about the earth,
What keeps it up, and the sky.
By listening to God's Word
One learns of islands, continents
And the regions of the netherworld.
By listening to God's Word
Death cannot affect you.
O Nanak, blessed for all time are those that worship,
By listening, sin and sorrow come to an end.

9

By listening to God's Word
One becomes like the gods
Shiva, Brahma and Indra.

By listening to God's Word
The lowest of the low praise Him.
By listening to God's Word
One learns the path of the yogi
And secrets of the body.
By listening to God's Word
One gets wisdom from the scriptures,
The Shastras, Smriti and Vedas.
O Nanak, blessed for all time are they that worship,
By listening, sin and sorrow come to an end.

10

Listening to God's Word brings
Truth, satisfaction and wisdom.
Listening to God's Word
Is like bathing at sixty-eight sacred places.
Listening to God's Word
And reading it, one is honoured.
Listening to God's Word
One grasps the essence of meditation.
O Nanak, blessed for all time are they who worship,
By listening, sin and sorrow come to an end.

11

By listening to God's Word
One throws oneself into the sea of virtue,
By listening to the Word
One becomes a religious leader,
Sufi teacher or ruler.

By listening to God's Word
Even the blind find their way.
By listening to God's Word
One can wade over the unfathomable;
O Nanak, blessed are they that worship, for all time
By listening, sin and sorrow come to an end.

12

No one can describe the state
Of one who believes.
Anyone who tries,
Lives to regret it.
There is no paper, pen
Or scribe who can describe
The state of the faithful.
Such is the Name of the Immaculate –
He who wants to know it, must have faith.

13

He who believes gets wisdom and understanding,
He who believes knows the world and all spheres.
He who believes does not come to grief,
He who believes does not fear death;
Such is the Name of the Immaculate –
He who wants to know it, must have faith.

14

There are no hindrances in the path
Of one who believes;
One who believes leaves the world

With honour and reputation intact;
He who believes does not lose his way
For faith has tied him to the law of Dharma;
Such is the Name of the Immaculate –
He who wants to know it must have faith.

15

He who believes finds the path to bliss
And saves his kith and kin;
Led by the Guru, the believer is saved
And can lead others across;
A believer, Nanak, does not wander and beg –
Such is the Name of the Flawless One,
To know Him one must believe.

16

Chosen leaders and saints
Are honoured in God's court;
While they grace the king's court
Their mind is on the Guru.

They think over what they are saying,
They know the Creator's deeds,
Born of His compassion
Is the bull who holds up the earth.

One who would learn the truth
Understands the load the bull must bear;
There are many worlds beyond this,

Many beyond them too;
Which power bears that burden?

Beings of various colours and name,
All written by an eternal flowing pen –
Who can write the story?
What a huge scroll that would be.

Which power, which enrapturing beauty,
Which gifts, who knows their extent?
The entire universe created with One Word,
A hundred thousand rivers started to flow;
Could I describe Your creative potential?
I am not worthy of being a sacrifice;
To do what pleases You is the best sacrifice
O You, the Eternal and Formless One.

17
Countless are they who pray,
Countless are they who love You,
Countless are they who pray to You,
Countless are they who try asceticism,
Countless are they who read the scriptures,
Countless are the yogis whose minds are detached,
Countless the disciples who wonder about
God's wisdom and virtues,
Countless are the holy, countless are the givers,
Countless are the warriors

Who match their strength with steel,
Countless are they who in silence
Focus their thoughts on You.
If only I could describe Your creativity.
I am not worthy of praising Your Might,
To do what pleases You is the only good,
O You, the Eternal and Formless One.

18
Countless are the fools, blinded by ignorance,
Countless are the thieves and cheaters,
Countless are they who impose their
Will with power,
Countless are the murderers who kill,
Countless are the sinners who go on sinning,
The liars who walk on with their lies,
Countless are they who eat what is unclean,
Countless are they who slander,
And bear on their heads the weight of their misdeeds –
Such, says Nanak, are the lowest of the low;
Could I describe your creative potential,
I who am not worthy of being sacrificed?
To do what pleases You is the best sacrifice,
O You, the Eternal and Formless One.

19
Countless names, countless places,
Inaccessible, inaccessible

Are the countless heavenly spheres –
Just calling them countless is a burden.

With letters and words Your Name is ingrained,
With letters and words we can praise You,
From the Word comes spiritual wisdom,
With words songs are sung that praise You,
With letters and words we can write and speak –
With words fate is written on one's forehead,
But the One who wrote all the words of fate,
No word is written on His forehead.

What He decides becomes our fate,
The creation is a revelation of His Name,
Without His Name there is no place;
Could I describe your creativity,
I who am not worthy of being sacrificed?
To do what pleases You is the best sacrifice,
O You, the Eternal and Formless One.

20
When hands, feet and other parts of the body are dirty,
Water can wash them clean;
When clothes are soiled
Soap can remove the stain;
But when the mind is muddied by sin,
It can only be cleansed by the breath of His Name.

Virtues and vices rest not on one's word alone
But on deeds repeated, which are written.
One reaps what one sows.
O Nanak, on God's command
One is saved or the soul wanders.

21

Pilgrimage, austerity, mercy, alms and charity
Are awarded even if as little as a sesame seed.
He who listens, believes in and loves the Name
Washes in the shrine that lies within us.

All virtues are Yours, I have none myself,
Without acting morally one cannot worship;
Blessed is the Creator,
The Primal One who is beautiful,
True and eternal, the heart's longing and joy.

Which time was it, which moment,
Which day, which date,
Which season, which month
When the earth was created?
Pandits don't know the time
Or it would have been in the Puranas,
The Qazis do not know it
While they write and copy the Quran,
Yogis know not the day or date,
Neither the month nor the season;

God, who created all on this earth,
Is the only one who knows.

How can I talk of You?
How can I praise You?
How can I describe You?
How can I get to know You?
O Nanak, all speak of Him,
One wiser than the other;
Great is the Master,
Great His Name,
Everything happens through His will,
O Nanak, he who claims he knows all
Is not praised by God later.

22

There are netherworld regions below the netherworld
And hundreds of thousands of heavenly kingdoms above;
The Vedas say you can search for them till you are tired and weary,
The holy scriptures say there are eighteen thousand worlds,
But actually there is but one universe;
If it were possible to describe it, someone would.
They who have tried have destroyed themselves doing it,
Nanak says, 'Say the Lord is great.'
Only He knows His own self.

23

Worshippers praise the Lord
But cannot grasp His form;

The stream and the river flow into the ocean
And do not know how vast it is;
Even kings and emperors with mountains of wealth
And oceans of riches
Are not as high as an ant
That keeps God's Name in mind.

24

Endless is His goodness, endless the praises of Him,
Endless are His works and His good deeds,
Endless His vision, endless His hearing,
His limits cannot be known,
His mind is a mystery that cannot be grasped,
The limits of His creations cannot be grasped,
Limits here and in life after death cannot be grasped.

Many strive to know His limits
But they cannot be found;
No one knows His limits –
The more you speak of it, the more there is to say;
Great is the Lord, high His heavenly home,
Higher than the highest is His Name.

One who is as high as God
Can grasp His exalted state;
Only He is great, He knows Himself.
O Nanak, with His glance of mercy
He gives us His blessing.

25

His blessings are so numerous, they cannot be recorded –
The Great Giver doesn't keep a sesame seed.
Many warriors stand and beg at His door
Many wait at His door, there is no number to them.

So many are destroyed because they are rotten,
So many take and take and refuse to admit they have received;
So many fools whose hunger never ceases,
So many that hunger and suffer and are beaten –
That too is a gift from You.

On your command, one is freed from slavery –
None but you has the power to do so;
Should a fool say something else,
He will have to swallow his words.

He knows our needs himself, He gives.
Few are they who admit this;
One who is blessed to praise God,
O Nanak, he is the king of kings.

26

Priceless are His virtues, priceless His trade,
Priceless His traders and priceless His treasure,
They that come to Him, they who trade with Him,
Priceless is their love for Him.
Priceless is their worship of Him,

Priceless His holy law,
Priceless is the holy court,
Priceless are His weights,
Priceless are His measures,
Priceless His magnanimity, priceless is His seal,
Priceless is His mercy, priceless His royal power;
More priceless than words can tell,
Those who speak of Him are struck dumb by love.

The Vedas speak, the Puranas speak,
The learned speak and give talks;
Brahma speaks, Indra speaks
So does Krishna and his lady loves,
Shiva speaks, the *siddhas* speak,
The many Buddhas You created speak.

Demons and gods speak,
But also warriors,
Ascetics and the servile speak,
Many speak and try to describe Him,
Many have spoken, got up and gone.

Were He to create countless new ones,
They would still not be able to describe Him;
The Word is as great as He desires it to be,
O Nanak, the true God knows.
He who tries to describe Him
Will be known as the biggest fool.

27
Where is the gate, where the house
Where You sit and look after everyone?
Where is it that the sound of song and music resounds
And countless musicians play all kinds of instruments?
So many ragas, so many singers.

There sings the wind, water and fire,
At the door stands Dharmaraj, the just Judge of Death;
The angels Chitra and Gupta record intentional and unintentional
deeds
And the just Judge, who sits in judgement, sings.

Shiva, Brahma and Devi of divine grace sing,
Indra on his throne sings with the gods at your door,
Ascetics sit and meditate, holy men wonder,
The pure, the peaceful and the content sing.
Fearless warriors sing,
Pandits and the learned who recite the Vedas sing,
With wise men from all ages.
The heavenly fair maidens who bewitch hearts
In this world, in paradise and the underworld, sing.
The heavenly jewels You have created sing,
In sixty-eight places of pilgrimage they sing.
Brave and mighty warriors sing,
The four sources of creation sing,
Planets, solar systems, galaxies
Created and placed by your hand sing.

Only those whom you love, who are drenched
By Your Grace, can praise you;
How many others there are I do not recall,
O Nanak, how shall I know them all?

He alone is always true, the Lord, and true is His Name,
He who made creation and will live for ever;
He created the earth with all colours, species diverse,
And looked upon what he had made;
Proof of His greatness.

What He decides will happen,
No orders can be given to Him –
For He is the king of kings
And Nanak must live as he decrees.

28

Let contentment be your earrings, humility your begging bowl,
Meditation the ash you cover your body with,
Let knowledge of death be your tattered robe,
And virginal purity your way of life;
Let faith in God be your staff,
Look at brotherhood of man as the yogi's highest order,
Know that when you tame your mind, you tame the whole world.
I bow down to Him,
The Primal One, the Pure Light,
Who is without beginning, without end –
One and only, for ever and ever.

29

Let spiritual wisdom be your food
And compassion your cook.
Nada, the unsung sound,
Resounds in every heart,
He alone is the highest master;
Empty rituals have no taste.

His will determines when we meet and part,
We get what is written by fate for us;
I bow down to Him,
The Primal One, the Pure Light,
Who is without beginning, without end –
One and only, for ever and ever.

30

A mother divine married, conceived and bore three gods –
One who created the world, one who sustains it and one who
destroys it,
But it is He who lets things happen as He wishes,
Such is His divine order.
He watches over everyone, but no one can see Him;
That is the biggest wonder.
I bow down to Him,
The Primal One, the Pure Light,
Who is without beginning, without end –
One and only, for ever and ever.

31

God's seat is in all spheres –
His treasure chamber in all worlds;
Our lot He decides once and for all.
The Creator watches over His creation
After creating it.
O Nanak, true is He,
True His work;
I bow down to Him,
The Primal one, the Pure Light
Who is without beginning and without end –
One and only, for ever and ever.

32

Had I a hundred thousand tongues, not one,
And a hundred thousand times twenty,
I would have with each tongue said
A hundred thousand times
One Name; the Master of the universe.
This is the way to our Lord's house,
The steps up to our Spouse,
To merge and be one with Him;
When they hear heavenly songs
Even insects that creep, wish to fly.

O Nanak, by His Grace can one merge
And be one with Him;
All else is vanity and false.

33
No energy to tell, nor to keep still,
No energy to ask for something, nor to give away anything,
No energy to live, nor the strength to die,
No strength to collect treasures and riches, or vanity,
No strength to force the mind into wisdom or thoughts,
No strength to find ways of escaping from the world;
He who has strength in his hands, let him see,
O Nanak, no one is below or above Him.

34
He who created night and day, weeks and seasons,
Wind, water, fire and underworld spheres;
In the middle of all this He created the earth
As a home of the law of Dharma,
Brought all species in all colours to it,
With names, without number and end.

By his deeds and actions shall a man be judged
For God himself is true, and true is His court,
Chosen leaders sit there to witness
And God gives them signs of His grace;
There they distinguish between mature and immature,
The good and the bad;
O Nanak, when you return home, you shall see this.

35
This is the realm of law,
Now I will speak of the realm of knowledge.
So much wind, water and fire,

So many Krishnas and Shivas,
So many Brahmas who create,
Forms of great beauty, decorated in many colours,
So many worlds, where one's deeds have consequences.

So many holy mountains to climb,
As Dhruv did, in order to learn;
So much thunder and lightning, so many moons and suns,
So many sages and wise men, so many masters of yoga,
So many goddesses of many a kind,
So many demigods and demons,
So many oceans of jewels,
So many forms of life, so many languages,
So many dynasties and kings,
So many who follow thoughts, so many who don't have judgement;
O Nanak, the number of His disciples knows no bounds.

36
Reason wins in the realm of wisdom,
And *nada* resounds among sounds and heavenly pleasures;
In the realm of humility, the Word is beauty;
Forms of beauty without compare are fashioned there.
All of this cannot be described –
He who tries will regret it,
Consciousness, understanding and intellect are shaped there;
It shapes the consciousness of wise and holy men.

37
In the realm of deeds, power reigns,
None other lives there

But brave and mighty warriors
Filled with God, and heavenly beauties
So beautiful that no words can describe them,
Sing of their glory.
They who have the Lord in their minds
Will not die or be deceived.
There disciples from many worlds live;
They celebrate, with minds filled with the true God.

In the realm of truth
The Formless One lives,
Who watches over His creation after He has made it,
With His glance of grace He gives pleasure;
Planets, solar systems, galaxies,
Of whose description there is no limit.

There are worlds beyond worlds that are
Created by Him;
As He ordains, so they do
All He beholds, thinks and ponders on,
O Nanak, is too hard to explain.

38
Let self-control be the furnace
And patience the goldsmith;
Let understanding be the anvil
And spiritual wisdom the hammer.

With the fear of God
Life is blown into the body's inner warmth,
In the melting pot of love
The Name's elixir melts
And the true coin of the Word is minted;
Such is the karma of those
The Lord looks upon with grace.
O Nanak, the generous Lord
Lifts and elevates them with His glance.

The wind is the Guru, water is the father,
The earth is mother to all,
Day and night are the two nurses
In whose lap the whole world plays.

Good deeds and bad,
The record is read out in front of the Lord of Dharma;
By one's deeds will some be pulled in
And others pushed away;
They who have meditated over the Name
And left us after finishing their work,
O Nanak, their faces glow in the court of the Lord;
Many are saved along with them.

GURU NanaK Dev: A TIMELine

1469: Guru Nanak, the first of the ten Sikh Gurus, was born at Rai Bhoi di Talwandi (present-day Nankana Sahib, Pakistan) near Lahore. Nanak was born on the third day of the month of Vaisakh, on Saturday, 15 April 1469. (If one follows the lunar calendar, the date changes annually but usually falls in November.) His birth is celebrated all over the world as Guru Nanak Gurpurab on Kartik Purnamasi, the full-moon day in the month of Kartik, in October–November.

His mother was Tripta Devi. Daulatan, a midwife, delivered the infant Nanak. His father, Kalyan Chand Das Bedi, belonged to the Hindu Khatri clan. He worked as the chief accountant of his village, and was commonly known as Kalu Mehta. Nanak's parents named him after his older sister Bibi Nanaki. Hardayal, a Hindu priest and astrologer, cast Nanak's horoscope.

1473: Mata Sulakhani was born to Mool Chand and Chando Rani.

1475: Bibi Nanaki, eleven years old, married Jai Ram, the *dewan* of Nawab Daulat Khan Lodi. However, she moved to Sultanpur to live with her husband only five years later when she was sixteen.

1481: Sacha Sauda. When Nanak was twelve, his father gave him money and sent him to the neighbouring town of Chuharkhana, asking him to make a real profit.

1485: Nanak met Mardana, a *mirasi* (a Muslim musician) who played the *rabab* and became Nanak's companion during his travels.

1485: Nanak's brother-in-law Jai Ram introduced him to Nawab Daulat Khan Lodi. When Daulat Khan got to know that Guru Nanak knew how to keep accounts and could read and write Persian, he appointed him as storekeeper at the Modi Khana (the state store) in Sultanpur.

1487: Sulakhani was married to Guru Nanak at Batala. This auspicious day is traditionally celebrated in Batala in Punjab during late August each year. Nanak was eighteen years old at the time of his marriage, Sulakhani must have been about fourteen.

1494: Sulakhani and Nanak's first son Sri Chand was born on 8 September. Sri Chand received enlightenment from Guru Nanak's teachings and went on to become the founder of the Udasi sect.

1497: Nanak and Sulakhani's second son Lakhmi Chand was born on 12 February.

1499: Sikh tradition states that Nanak went missing at the age of thirty, and was presumed to have drowned after going for his morning bath to a local river called the Kali Bein.

1500: Nanak decided to start his sacred mission to spread the holy message of peace and compassion to all mankind. Although married with two children, Nanak set out on a series of spiritual journeys through India, Tibet and Arabia, which lasted more than two decades. He studied and debated with the learned men he met along the way and as his ideas took shape he began to teach a new route to spiritual fulfilment and a good life.

1506: Nanak returned home to Talwandi and visited his parents after the first Udasi (or trip) to east India.

1508: When Nanak set out on another of his long trips in 1508, it was to promote his mission. This Udasi focused primarily on visiting Hindu places of pilgrimage.

1519: Babur came to Lahore at the invitation of Daulat Khan Lodi.

1522: Nanak's mother Mata Tripta passed away at Talwandi just as he returned from one of his journeys, and he was able to organize her funeral. He settled down at Kartarpur and spent the rest of his life there. There was daily *kirtan* and the institution of *langar* (community kitchen) was introduced.

1524: Babur started for Lahore but found that Daulat Khan Lodi had been driven out by forces sent by Ibrahim Lodi. When Babur arrived at Lahore, the Lodi army marched out and the former's army was routed. In retaliation, Babur burned Lahore for two days, then marched to Dipalpur, placing Alam Khan, another rebel uncle of the Lodi's, as governor. Alam Khan was quickly overthrown and fled to Kabul. Babur then supplied Alam Khan with troops; they later joined Daulat Khan Lodi and together with about 30,000 troops, they besieged Ibrahim Lodi at Delhi.

1539: Nanak appointed Bhai Lehna as the successor Guru, renaming him Guru Angad, meaning 'one's very own' or 'part of one.' Shortly after proclaiming Bhai Lehna as his successor, Guru Nanak died in Kartarpur on 22 September.

1545: Mata Sulakhani expired six years after Guru Nanak at Kartarpur on the banks of the river Ravi, where she spent the last years of her life.

Bonus Quiz: How Well Do You Know Guru Nanak Dev?

1. Guru Nanak Gurpurab marks the birth anniversary of Guru Nanak. Which religion considers it a sacred festival?
   a) Hinduism
   b) Islam
   c) Sikhism
   d) Christianity

2. What is Guru Nanak Gurpurab also known as?
   a) Prakash Utsav
   b) Rang Utsav
   c) Kirpa Utsav
   d) Kartik Utsav

3. When was Guru Nanak born?
   a) 1396
   b) 1432
   c) 1459
   d) 1469

4. Guru Nanak Dev was born at Rai Bhol di Talwandi in the present Shekhupura District of Pakistan. What is the current name of his birthplace?
   a) Punja Sahib
   b) Nankana Sahib
   c) Bangla Sahib
   d) Rakab Gunj Sahib

5. Guru Nanak Gurpurab falls on Purnima, the day of the full moon, in which month of the Indian calendar?

   a) Kartik

   b) Agrahayana

   c) Ashvini

   d) Pausha

6. On the day of Gurpurab, the celebrations start early in the morning, between 4 and 5 a.m. What is this time of day called?

   a) Prabhat Samay

   b) Amrit Vela

   c) Savera Vela

   d) Subah Vela

7. What is the special community lunch arranged at Gurudwaras by volunteers called?

   a) Langar

   b) Bhojan

   c) Bhojanalaya

   d) Khidmat

8. The holy book of the Sikhs, the Guru Granth Sahib, is taken out two days before the birth anniversary of Guru Nanak and is read without a break. What is this called?

   a) Akhand Path

   b) Ardas

   c) Akhand Ardas

   d) Amrit Path

9. In which year did Nanak and Mardana go on the first trip or Udasi?

   a) 1500

b) 1459

c) 1506

d) 1511

10. Where was the first Udasi?

a) East India

b) South India and Sri Lanka

c) Singapore

d) Afghanistan

11. In which language were Guru Nanak's teachings first recorded?

a) Pali

b) Hindi

c) Urdu

d) Gurmukhi

12. Nanak would go and bathe in a river in Sultanpur. Which river was it?

a) The Ravi

b) The Sutlej

c) The Indus

d) The Bein

13. During his Udasis, which companion did Nanak always travel with?

a) Lalo

b) Mardana

c) Mata Sulakhani

d) Lakhmi Chand

14. When Nanak went down to the river in Sultanpur and disappeared for three days, how old was he?

a) 16

b) 22

c) 28

d) 30

15. What did Nanak consider true profit?

   a) Making more money than he had spent.

   b) Getting a good price for his goods.

   c) Feeding the hungry and serving people.

   d) Coming home with lots of money.

16. Nanak and Mardana were childhood friends.

   a) False. They met in Talwandi, but Mardana was much older than Nanak.

   b) True. They went to school together.

   c) True. They would graze their buffaloes together.

   d) True. Mardana lived next door and their parents were old friends.

17. Why did Nanak have problems when he was the manager of the Nawab's granary?

   a) He couldn't keep track of the money.

   b) They ran out of wheat.

   c) He never gave anyone anything more than thirteen measures of grain.

   d) Someone heard him saying 'Sab tera' and thought he was not counting the measures correctly.

18. Nanak and Mardana used to play and sing together. They composed many hymns in several ragas that are sung to this day. Which instrument did Mardana play?

   a) The harmonium

   b) The pakhawaj

   c) The ektara

   d) The rabab

19. Nanak always composed his songs using Raga Asavari.

    a) No, he used many different ragas, of which Asavari was one.

    b) No, he liked Rabindra Sangeet.

    c) No, he was very fond of Carnatic ragas he had learned when he went to south India.

    d) No, he was influenced by Tibetan folk songs.

20. Nanak got the job at the Modi Khana in Sultanpur because the Nawab was impressed with his knowledge of languages. Which language did he need to know for his accounts?

    a) Punjabi

    b) Hindi

    c) Urdu

    d) Persian

21. How many spiritual journeys or Udasis did Guru Nanak undertake?

    a) Three

    b) Four

    c) Five

    d) Six

22. When they were in Bengal, Nanak and Mardana went to bed outdoors, hungry and thirsty because:

    a) the villagers in the village they came to were at a wedding.

    b) there was no food to be had.

    c) the villagers were very inhospitable.

    d) the villagers thought they were thieves.

23. Mardana and Nanak visited a carpenter in Sayyadpur. What was his name?

    a) Lalo

    b) Lado

    c) Malik Bhago

    d) Manoj

24. Why did the Sultan of Aminabad call Lalo over to his palace?

    a) He wanted some new furniture.

    b) He knew Nanak was there and he wanted to listen to some music.

    c) His son was ill and he wanted Lalo to find a cure.

    d) He wanted Lalo to say some prayers.

25. Guru Nanak was critical of some of the social ills of the time. Which of the following was he specially involved with?

    a) He felt the caste system was wrong because all people are equal.

    b) He felt there was no good system of collecting taxes.

    c) He did not like the judges and the legal system.

    d) He did not like the education system.

26. Nanak wanted people to have faith in one Omnipotent God because:

    a) it was simpler than remembering many gods.

    b) Babur had invaded India.

    c) he was against conventions.

    d) he felt that if one meditated and lived honestly, one would awaken the divine in all human beings and people would become one with God.

27. How did Nanak and Mardana travel to faraway lands?

    a) By plane

    b) By ship

    c) In a horse and carriage

    d) On foot

28. Who invited Babur to invade India?

    a) Ibrahim Lodi

    b) Daulat Khan Lodi

    c) Rana Sanga

    d) Shah Jahan

29. Where was Nanak when Babur invaded Punjab?

    a) Patiala

    b) Batala

    c) Sayyadpur

    d) Talwandi

30. When Nanak was arrested by the Mughals, what did he do?

    a) He resisted

    b) He went to prison with Mardana and was made to grind corn.

    c) He escaped on the way to prison.

    d) He started to meditate.

31. Why would Nanak's parents despair of him at times?

    a) Because he was rebellious and rejected conventions.

    b) Because he spoke rudely to them.

    c) Because they wanted him to stay in town and look after their cows and buffaloes.

    d) Because the neighbours gossiped about him.

32. Nanak wore the robes of an ascetic and believed in living the life of a hermit.

    a) He felt one could lead a family life without being materialistic.

    b) He couldn't afford to buy clothes so he wore a tattered robe.

    c) There were no shops when he went on his journeys, so he could not buy new clothes.

    d) No, he wanted to go away and live in a forest.

33. What does the word 'Haumai' mean?

    a) I am

    b) Bliss

c) Meditation

d) Grace

34. What is 'Satsang'?

a) A community meal.

b) Contemplation and meditation on God's name, in the company of other devoted people.

c) Singing hymns

d) Cooking food for followers

35. What is 'Kirtan'?

a) Community discussions

b) Singing hymns

c) Meditating

d) Eating together

36. Where is the Gurudwara Panja Sahib located?

a) Hasan Abdal

b) Patiala

c) Kapurthala

d) Nabha

37. In which place did Nanak squeeze milk and blood out of bread?

a) Lahore

b) Talwandi

c) Sayyadpur

d) Baghdad

38. Who are the five thieves?

a) Pride, Anger, Greed, Attachment and Lust

b) Greed, Hunger, Lust, Black Magic, Anger

c) Contentment, Charity, Kindness, Positive Energy and Humility

d) The five senses

39. Where is Batala situated?

a) Andhra Pradesh

b) Arunachal Pradesh

c) Nagaland

d) Punjab

40. When did Nanak move to Kartarpur?

a) 1485

b) 1506

c) 1511

d) 1522

41. How many verses by Guru Nanak does the Adi Granth, which later came to be known as the Guru Granth Sahib, contain?

a) 300

b) 563

c) 257

d) 974

42. Which Guru succeeded Guru Nanak?

a) Guru Arjun Dev

b) Guru Gobind Singh

c) Guru Angad Dev

d) Guru Amar Das

43. Did Guru Nanak ask people to convert to Sikhism and become Sikhs?

a) He asked people to come to Kartarpur and join a Sikh commune.

b) He never asked his listeners to follow him. He asked Muslims to be good Muslims and Hindus to be good Hindus.

c) He asked them to convert to Sikhism.

d) During this time, although his followers still remained Hindu, Muslim, or of the religion to which they were born, they became known as the Guru's disciples, or Sikhs.

44. How many Gurus are there in Sikhism?

a) 12

b) 9

c) 10

d) 5

45. Which relative of Guru Nanak's became a spiritual figure in her own right?

a) Mata Tripta

b) Bibi Nanaki

c) Bibi Sulakhani

d) Bibi Lalwanti

ANSWERS: 1C, 2A, 3D, 4B, 5A, 6B, 7A, 8A, 9A, 10A, 11D, 12D, 13B, 14D, 15C, 16A, 17D, 18D, 19A, 20D, 21B, 22C, 23A, 24C, 25A, 26D, 27D, 28B, 29C, 30B, 31A, 32A, 33A, 34B, 35B, 36A, 37C, 38A, 39D, 40D, 41D, 42C, 43D, 44C (BESIDES THE 10 GURUS, THE GURU GRANTH SAHIB IS ALSO REVERED AS A GURU); 45B.

Acknowledgements

I am indebted as always to my editor Vatsala Kaul Banerjee.

I am also extremely grateful for advice that Anand Singh Bawa and Jugneeta Sudan gave while I was translating the Japji Sahib.

For inspiration, I would like to thank Knut Jacobsen, who got me interested in the Guru Granth Sahib twelve years ago when he asked me to translate hymns from the Adi Granth to Norwegian.

I would also like to thank Ankita Rana at Hachette India for her hawk-eyed copyediting and help in getting this book together.

Any mistakes are solely my own.

Select Bibliography

Dhillon, Harish. *Janamsakhis: Ageless Stories, Timeless Vision*. Hay House Publishers, New Delhi, 2015.

Shackle, C. *A Guru Nanak Glossary*. Heritage Publishers, New Delhi, 1995.

Singh, Gopal (translated and annotated by). *Sri Guru Granth Sahib*, Vols. 1–4. Allied Publishers Pvt Limited, New Delhi, 2002.

Macauliffe, M.A (1909). *The Sikh Religion: Its Gurus, Sacred Writings and Authors*. (Vols. 1–6). Cambridge University Press, New York, 2013.

McDermott, Rachel Fell, Gordon, Leonard A., Embree, Ainslie T., Pritchett, Francis W., Dalton, Dennis. *The Sources of Indian Tradition*. Penguin, New Delhi, 2014.

Singh, Khushwant (1963). *A History of the Sikhs: 1469-1839 Vol.1 (2nd ed.)*. Oxford University Press, New Delhi, 1999.

Singh, Khushwant. *The Japji and the Rehras*. Rupa Publications India, New Delhi, 2013.

Singh, Khushwant. *Hymns of Guru Nanak*. Orient Blackswan, 1991.

Singh, Roopinder. *Guru Nanak, His Life and Teachings*. Rupa & Co., Delhi, 2004.

Web Resources

Singh Baljit, Singh, Inderjeet. *Travels of Guru Nanak* (Activity Book). Sikh Foundation, New Delhi, www.gurmatveechar.com

https://www.sikhiwiki.org/index.php/Guru_Nanak

http://www.sikhnet.com/

http://www.sikh-history.com/sikhhist/gurus/nanak1.html